Anthony Poulton-Smith
EAST SUSSEX
PLACE NAMES

First published in Great Britain in 2012 by The Derby Books Publishing Company Limited, 3 The Parker Centre, Derby, DE21 4SZ.

© Anthony Poulton-Smith, 2012

ISBN 978-1-78091-016-1

EAST SUSSEX PLACE NAMES

Contents

Introduction

For years the history of England was based on the Roman occupation. In recent years we have come to realise the influence of the Empire did not completely rewrite British history, indeed there was already a thriving culture in England well before the birth of Christ. When the Romans left our shores in the fifth century the arrival of the Anglo-Saxons was thought to herald a time of turmoil, yet they brought the culture and language which forms the basis of modern England. Later the arrival of the Norsemen saw their influence and the same is true of our place names, the vast majority of settlement names in East and West Sussex are derived from the Saxon/Old English or Old Scandinavian tongues. There are also the topographical features such as rivers and hills which still have the names given to them by the Celts of the pre-Roman era.

Ostensibly place names are simple descriptions of the location, or of the uses and the people who lived there. In the pages that follow, an examination of the origins and meanings of the names in East Sussex will reveal all. Not only will we see Saxon and Scandinavian settlements, but Celtic rivers and hills, Roman roads and even Norman French landlords who have all contributed to the evolution, to some degree, of the names we are otherwise so familiar with.

Not only are the basic names discussed but also districts, hills, streams, fields, roads, lanes, streets and public houses. Road and street names are normally of more recent derivation, named after those who played a significant role in the development of a town or revealing what existed in the village before the developers moved in. The benefactors who provided housing and employment in the 18th and 19th centuries are often forgotten, yet their names live on in the name found on the sign at the end of the street and often have a story to tell.

Pub names are almost a language of their own. Again they are not named arbitrarily but are based on the history of the place and can open a new window on the history of our towns and villages.

Defining place names of all varieties can give an insight into history which would otherwise be ignored or even lost. In the ensuing pages we shall examine 2,000 plus years of East Sussex.

Anthony Poulton-Smith

Alciston

Domesday lists this name as Alsistone in 1086, a record pointing to a Saxon personal name and Old English *tun* and telling of 'the farmstead of a man called Aelfsige or Ealhsige'.

Tilton is found all over England; although the suffix *tun* is common to all, the preceding Saxon personal name has several possibilities. Here the origin is 'the farmstead of a man called Tella'.

The Rose Cottage Inn took its name from the building's existing address, itself needing no explanation. The road outside this pub is closed on Good Friday each year when it becomes the venue for a traditional skipping contest.

Alfriston

First seen as Alvricestone in the *Domesday* record of 1086, this is derived from a Saxon personal name and Old English *tun* and tells of 'the farmstead of a man called Aelfric'.

Minor names here include Follers Manor House, a name which was erroneously transferred when the map was redrawn. It seems the original surname was either Tollers or Tollards. Hindover comes from *ofer* to refer to 'the high bank of land'.

Winton is a somewhat shortened version of the original where a Saxon personal name was suffixed by *ing tun* to record this as 'the farmstead associated with a man called Wiga'.

Alfriston's pubs include the George Inn, a patriotic name referring to St George, the patron saint of England. Named from a minor place name, the Wingrove Inn was a family home from the middle of the 19th century describing 'the grove near a meadow or pasture' from *winn graefe*.

Ye Olde Smugglers Inn is indeed what it says, an old haunt of those who earned a living through smuggling contraband into the country. As an inn the building dates back to at least 1385, however, it was during the tenure of Stanton Collins that this building acquired its many secret nooks and crannies, cubbyholes and hideaways. During the Napoleonic Wars Alfriston enjoyed sudden prosperity, the troops stationed nearby brought and spent their pay here – some of it went on ale and some on pleasures of the flesh. After the threat of invasion disappeared in 1815 the troops disappeared, leaving Alfriston penniless. The locals soon gave in to the temptation of earning a crust through smuggling, with Stanton Collins certainly providing encouragement.

Without further evidence the Star Inn would probably be thought to show a pub standing on church land, the image representing the Virgin Mary. For once we have a quite detailed history of this 13th-century inn. Until at least 1520 it was run by the monks of Battle Abbey, furthermore it was formerly known as the Star of Bethlehem. This earlier name shows it was representative of the birth of Christ and thus their chosen religion of Christianity.

Arlington

Found as Erlington in 1086, the *Domesday* record shows this to be a Saxon personal name and Old English *ing tun*, telling of 'the farmstead associated with a man called Eorla'.

Chilver Bridge is from Old English *ceosol ford*, a reminder this was 'the shingly or pebbly ford'. Michelham comes from *micel ham*, Old English for 'the great homestead'. Nothing spectacular but simply larger than those normally found in the Saxon era. Raylands speaks of itself as 'the land by the well-watered place'. From Old English *inga ham* and a Saxon personal name, Sessingham began as 'the homestead of the family or followers of a man called Seaxa'.

Ashburnham

Domesday records the name as Esseborne in 1086, with a later record of Esburneham in 1211. Here Old English *aesc* is suffixed by either *ham* or *hamm* giving 'the homestead by the ash trees' or 'the ash trees at the hemmed-in land' respectively.

The local pub is most appropriately known as the Ash Tree Inn.

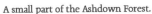
A small part of the Ashdown Forest.

Ashdown Forest

A document of 1207 gives this name as Essendon, a name from Old English *aescen dun* and describing 'the hill where ash trees grow'.

B

Barcombe

Domesday's listing of Bercham and the 12th century record Berecampe show this is from Old English *bere camp* and describes 'the enclosed land used for barley'. Barcombe Cross is nearby, a hamlet which has been an overspill since at least the Middle Ages when many of the population were evacuated here to escape an outbreak of the bubonic plague.

Local names begin with Balneath Manor House, the suffix derived from *heath* and speaking of 'the heath associated with a man called Balla'. Caveridge features another personal name, here with *hrycg* and giving 'the ridge of a man called Cafa'. Spithurst features the element *hyrst* 'wooded hill'; here the first element has been corrupted and spoke of 'the split wooded hill'. Here the 'split' informs us of a path or way passing right through it.

Two pubs are found here, the Royal Oak a reminder of the escape of Charles II and the day he hid in the branches of an oak tree to escape his pursuers. Since it was built in 1790 the Anchor Inn has stood on the banks of the River Ouse, thus the name is a reference to its location.

Battle

Famously this place took its name from the abbey built here to commemorate the site of what has become known as the Battle of Hastings in 1066. Listed as La Batailge in *Domesday*, this name comes from the Old French *bataille* or the '(place at) the battle'.

Powdermill Lane can be traced back to 1676 when the first gunpowder mill was built in Battle. This was land owned by the abbey when John Hammond was granted permission to open his mill. In 1722 Daniel Defoe wrote of his visit to Battle where he was particularly taken by 'what must be the finest gunpowder produced anywhere in Europe'. However, this ended in 1847 when the licence was not renewed as the Duke of Cleveland was tired of the many accidents, including one time when over 15 tons of gunpowder exploded after being left in the oven for too long.

Many of the minor place names here may well have been in use before the battle, although records before 1066 are few. Bathurst Wood, the suffix from *hyrst* added to a personal name as 'the wooded hill of a man called Boda'. Branshill Farm occupies land once known for being 'the hill covered with brambles'. Duckreed Wood takes the name of the 'streamlet frequented by ducks'. Ibrook Wood is also an old stream name, here 'the brook where yew trees grow'.

Rat Farm was never infested by rodents, at least that was not the reason for the place name. Here the origin is Old English *ryt*, which hardly paints a much more attractive picture of 'the place with rubbish for burning'. Milestone Wood is self-explanatory, although for once we know the milestone it refers to, one marking a distance of 55 miles from London.

Locals will enjoy a drink in the Red Lion public house, still likely the most common pub name in the land. As with many colour/animal combinations, this is heraldic. There are two possible origins here; either this shows a link to Scotland or to John of Gaunt, the most powerful man in England in the 14th century. Gaunt is an anglicised 'Ghent', where this Duke of Lancaster and member of the House of Plantagenet was born. While he never ruled England in name, as the third son of Edward III he exercised his influence over his nephew, Richard II, his male heirs, Kings Henry IV, Henry V and Henry VI, and female heirs Queen Philippa of Portugal and Queen Catherine of Castille and all the subsequent generations. One cannot ignore a particular illegitimate line known by the surname Beaufort, a line legitimized by a decree, with the proviso they had no claims on the English throne. However, they were crowned in Scotland from 1437 and thus, from 1603, also England when the two countries were ruled by the House of Stuart. Hence the image of the Red Lion came to Scotland from John of Gaunt.

There can be few pubs in the land which have a more obvious origin than the 1066. It may also be unique in being named after a year. William ordered the building of the abbey after his victory, hence the naming of the Abbey Hotel. No surprise to find Ye Olde Kings Head features an image of William the Conqueror, although it more likely shows support for the monarchy in general as indeed does the Kings Arms.

The Lamb Inn is a religious sign, the reference being to Jesus Christ, the Lamb of God. Another possibly religious image is seen in the Bull Inn, this being representative of the papacy. However, it was also used by many families and bodies, or it may simply refer to a favourite animal. The same applies to the Black Horse Inn, probably heraldic but the animal cannot be ruled out. The George Hotel is a patriotic name, the reference being to St George, patron saint of England.

From Roman times the chequer board has been used as a pub sign, showing a board game similar to draughts was played within. Later the sign was used to show a money lender, the word still associated with finances in the shape of the Chancellor of the Exchequer. Seen since the 16th century, the Plough Inn retains its popularity despite the original idea of attracting agricultural workers not being anywhere near as appropriate today.

Once there was an opportunity for your horse to be shod as you enjoyed refreshment at the Blacksmiths Inn. Perhaps the Squirrel Inn gets its name from the small arboreal rodent, although an heraldic image is not out of the question. However, no doubt the Netherfield Arms takes its name from the minor place name describing 'the lower open land'.

Beachy Head

The earliest surviving record of this name dates from 1279 as Beuchef. This name comes from Old French *beau chef* and describes 'the beautiful headland', later the addition of Head says the same thing as the suffix. The name is shared by the pub, the Beachy Head.

The highest chalk cliff in Britain, rising to a height of 530ft, it certainly merits its name. Sadly this great height and its excellent views also make it one of the most notorious suicide spots in the world. With an average of around 20 deaths each year, only the Aokigahara Woods in Japan and the Golden Gate Bridge in San Francisco attract more suicides.

In 1831 the headland was proving too costly a danger to shipping and a lighthouse was erected on the headland to the west. The Belle Tout Lighthouse, the name suggests everything is beautiful, became operational in 1834 but owing to its position on the cliff tops, fog and clouds could hide the light and a second lighthouse was built in the sea below Beachy Head and shone its light from 1902. At least one of these lighthouses was permanently manned until it became fully automated in 1983.

Beckley

Documented as Beccanlea at the end of the ninth century, this name comes from a Saxon personal name and Old English *leah* and describes 'the woodland clearing of a man called Becca'.

Locally we find Kitchenour, the Saxon name followed by Old English *ora* and telling of 'the place of a man called Cycci at the slope'. The suffix *leah* follows the personal name at Ludley Farm, this telling of 'the woodland clearing of a man called Ladda'. Another man's name is seen at Methersham, here followed by *hamm* to tell of 'the hemmed-in land of a man called Maethhere'.

Here the Royal Oak public house marks the escape of Charles II following defeat at the Battle of Worcester in 1651. As a name it gained popularity at the Restoration of the Monarchy a decade later, when the King's birthday of 29 May was declared Royal Oak Day. This was once a public holiday, when children would wear sprigs of oak leaves and possibly oak apples too. Those who failed to follow the custom were likely to find themselves thrashed with bunches of nettles. The Rose and Crown is another patriotic name, the rose representative of England and the crown its monarch.

Beckley once had a furnace, built in 1578 it was a small part of the extensive Wealden iron industry. A significant proportion of the iron made in the country came from the Weald, siderite or iron stone being found in readily workable quantities across the region while the many trees provided charcoal for the fire. These were early days and quality of the iron differed widely. However, experienced smelters rescued much of the iron from scrap by mixing the various grades to produce metal which was used in bars and in the production of cannon. With bellows powered by a watermill, production continued at Beckley until 1770. By this time much of the Weald's iron production had ceased as coke, a derivative of coal, was used instead of charcoal and the region has no coal seams.

Beddingham

Listed as Beadyngham in the ninth century and as Bedingeham in *Domesday*, this comes from a Saxon personal name and Old English *inga hamm* and tells us this was 'the hemmed in land of the family or followers of a man called Beada'.

Before Asham House was built, the place name derived from *assa ham* already existed. This described 'the homestead where donkeys were raised'.

Berwick

The only early record of note is from *Domesday* as Beruice. Despite the shortage of forms this is certainly from Old English *bere wic*, understood as 'the farm specialising in the production of barley'.

Bexhill

Seen as Bixlea in 772 and as Bexelei in 1086, this represents Old English *byxe leah* or 'the woodland clearing where box trees grow'.

Street names tell their own history of a place. One of the most commonly found is the developer. Here Allan Way, Amanda Close, Angela Close, Christine Close, Diana Close, Ian Close, and Lesley Close all took first names of the family.

Those in residence are always an excellent choice for their names are already here and unlikely to be controversial. For example Alfray Road is after local ironmaster Thomas Alfray. Lord Astor of Hever gave his name to Gavin Astor Close. George Gillham was the leader of the Little Common gang of smugglers said to have lived at what is now known as Gillham Wood Road.

Ingrams Avenue was cut on the land once a part of Ingrams Farm. Mitten Road was named after a local farmer. Popps Lane and Preson Road similarly recall Popps Farm and Preston Farm. Saxby Road immortalises the name of a local family.

Barrack Road was the site of barracks for soldiers, built in 1804 for the Napoleonic Wars. Turkey Road was once an old turkey farm. Winceby Close is on land which was once a part of the Winceby House private school. Little Twitten features the Sussex dialect word for 'an alleyway'. Martletts gets its name from the heraldic name for the swift and is used in the Sussex coat of arms.

Local officials are often a favourite and there are numerous examples in Bexhill. Ashby Close is named after Alderman Ashby; Alderman F.J. Bending gave his name to Bending Crescent; Bodle Crescent honours Alderman T. Bodle; E.W.C. Bowrey served as mayor in 1923, hence the naming of Bowrey Place; Buxton Drive remembers Alderman F.C. Buxton; Alderman Mrs Claxton gave her name to Claxton Road; Alderman F.C. Cooper is remembered by Cooper Drive; while Courthope Drive commemorates the work of the Honourable Daphnae Courthope, who served as chairwoman of East Sussex County Council for 20 years from 1940.

Cuthbert Close is after Alderman W.N. Cuthbert, Justice of the Peace; Davis Close recalls Alderman A.H. Davis; Gibb Close is after Councillor J. Gibb; Meads Road remembers Alderman Mrs C.I. Meads MBE and Justice of the Peace; Morgan Close recalls Councillor Morgan; Mayor J.A. Paton is commemorated by Paton Road; Sewell Avenue remembers the work of Councillor R.C. Sewell; and the name of Councillor Stevens is on the sign in Stevens Close.

Not only local government but national, with Brookfield Road named after Colonel A.M. Brookfield, who served as member of parliament. Beeching Close and Beeching Road were cut on the old goods yard site. It was the closure of this part of the railway which freed this land for development. These closures blamed on the infamous Doctor Richard Beeching, who headed the government enquiry into the profitability of the railways.

Minor names here include Barnhorne, which describes 'the corner of land of a man called Byrna'. Cooden Down also features as a Saxon personal name, although here the place was probably named for him in his absence, most likely posthumously, as the '(place) of the family or followers of a man called Coda'. Gotham, note the pronunciation should be 'goat-ham', is from a Saxon personal name and Old English *hamm* to give 'the hemmed in land where goats are reared'.

Hurchington has three elements, a Saxon personal name preceding Old English *inga tun* to give 'the farmstead of the family or followers of a man called Herric'. Pebsham Farm also features a Saxon name, here speaking of 'the *ham* or homestead of a man called Pyppel'. Picknill Green, where the *grene* is a later Middle English addition of obvious meaning, again features a Saxon name, this time with the suffix *glind* to give 'the enclosure of a man called Pica'. Again the village green is added to the basic Old English name in Sidley Green, which was located at 'the wide woodland clearing'. Worsham Farm has its suffix from *ham* and speaks of 'the homestead of a man called Wyrtel'.

Pub names of Bexhill begin with the Devonshire Arms; the Stanley family, dukes of Devonshire, being major landholders in the country. The Rose and Crown is also symbolic, this being the house of a patriot where the rose represents England and the crown its monarchy.

Any New Inn should be thought of as 'newer' as few examples could ever be seen as 'new' today. The Sportsman originally showed games were played or organised within. A former official ringing his bell with shouts of "Oyez, oyez" prior to making public announcements may have been a common sight outside the Town Crier. Only a few miles distant the Norman fortification at Herstmonceux was the inspiration for the name of the Castle public house.

In March 1963 the big news was the major shake-up of Britain's railway network. The front pages carried images of a gentleman sporting a Hitler-style moustache alongside the shocking details of a salary emphasised to be two and a half times that of the prime minister. Almost 50 years later the name of Doctor Beeching is still up there with Quisling and seen almost as a traitor to his nation. Yet situated on land released by the railway we find the premises called Doctor Beechings.

The Wheatsheaf is taken from the coat of arms of the Brewers Company or the Worshipful Company of Bakers. Coming from the Feilding family is the pub known as the Denbigh, they being earls of Denbigh. With its sign showing the origin of a lighthouse boat of the same name is the Royal Sovereign. A family who became earls of Chichester gave their name to the Pelham Hotel. While the Bell Hotel has a name showing it is associated with the church.

Bexhill is hardly the first name to come to mind when speaking of international motorsport, yet in 1902 some distinguished names brought their prized vehicles to the coast for a series of races. More than 200 competitors raced in a series of time trials over a straight course running down from Galley Hill. The competitors also raced head to head in the opposite direction. These scenes attracted thousands of spectators who must have been more than a little scared by the rumbling felt through the ground as the racers thundered past them at more than 50mph. Not a great rate today but in 1902 this was more than four times the national speed limit of 12mph. Perhaps planners may consider using some of the names associated with these races in their new developments.

Bishopstone

From Old English *biscop tun* and describing 'the farmstead of the bishop'. This name is recorded in *Domesday* as Biscopestone.

The church of St Andrew here is likely the oldest in the county. The present rebuild dates from 1200 but there is good reason to believe parts date from at least the eighth century. Inside the church is a memorial to former clergyman and poet James Hurdis, who was born in Bishopstone in 1763. Hurdis became Professor of Poetry at Oxford University in 1793 but during his frequent visits to his native county would compensate shepherds with a few coins when he freed the caged songbirds they had trapped and intended to sell to supplement their small income.

Blatchington, East

Records of this name include Blechinton in 1169. Derived from a Saxon personal name and Old English *ing tun*, this tells of 'the farmstead associated with a man called Blaecca'.

Blatchington, West

Listed as Blacintona in 1121, again here is a Saxon personal name and Old English *ing tun* and 'the farmstead associated with a man called Blaecca'.

Bodiam

From a Saxon personal name and Old English *ham* this name refers to 'homestead of a man called Boda'. The name is recorded as Bodeham in the *Domesday* record of 1086.

Boreham

From Old English *bor ham* or *bor hamm*, this name describes 'the homestead by a hill' and 'the hemmed in land by the hill' respectively. The name is recorded as Borham in the 12th century.

Brede

Seen in a document from 1161 as Brade, here the Old English element *braedu* tells of 'the broad stretch of land'. The River Brede is named from the place, an example of back-formation.

Arndale Bridge gets its name from the family named Arnold, recorded here by 1434. Chitcombe is a combination of a Saxon personal name with Old English *cumb* and refers to 'the valley of a man called Citta'. Snathurst Wood is from the same tongue, here the rare word *snad* and the common suffix *hyrst* come together to refer to 'the isolated wooded hill'.

Brighton

This name is found as Bristelmestune in the *Domesday* record of 1086. Today the form is very much abbreviated from the original 'farmstead of a man called Beorhthelm'.

Old Steine took its name from the vast number of oddly shaped stones which were dug from here.

The streets of Brighton can be divided into various groups or categories, the following would not qualify as themes as they are not in one region but scattered throughout the area. There are those featuring royal christian names. Albert Road remembers Prince Albert, consort of Queen Victoria who is seen in Victoria Road and Queen Victoria Avenue. Queen Alexandra Avenue recalls the wife and consort of Edward VII, the latter giving his name to Edward Street. Leopold Street is named after Prince Leopold, Duke of Albany. Alfred Road remembers Prince Alfred, Duke of Saxe-Coburg and Gotha. Charles Road is named after the current Prince of Wales. George Street is probably after George III, while his wife and consort Queen Charlotte of Mecklenburg-Strelitz gave a name to Charlotte Street. George's father, Prince of Wales, gave a name to Frederick Street, while George's son, the future William IV, is seen in the name of William Street.

Royal dukedoms have formed another category, seen in Cambridge Road, Clarence Square, Cumberland Road, Gloucester Road, Sussex Road, and York Road. Royal houses are represented and have produced Brunswick Place and Hanover Terrace, both relating to the monarchs ruling in Britain from 1714 to 1901 and referred to as the House of Hanover.

Royal residences have given names to roads, too. Carlton Terrace recalls Carlton House, home of the Prince Regent from 1783. Kensington Palace, home to a great succession of royals since the 17th century, is seen in both Kensington Place and Kensington Street. Kew Palace, in the grounds of Kew Gardens, was home to the Levett family of Sussex, thus another link to Kew Street. St James's

Brighton's Pier.

Street is from St James's Palace, still the official residence of the monarchy although none have lived there since George III. Predictably Windsor Castle was the basis for Windsor Street, the castle is the longest occupied royal residence in Europe.

Not only royal dukes have given names to streets but those associated with non-royals, too. Examples include Argyle Road, Beaufort Terrace, both Bedford Place and Bedford Square, Buckingham Road and also Buckingham Place, Devonshire Place, Grafton Street, Hamilton Road, Manchester Street, Norfolk Square and Norfolk Road, Portland Road and Portland Place, Richmond Road, Somerset Street, Sutherland Road, and finally Wellington Street and Wellington Road.

It is not necessary to be a king, queen or duke to have a road named after you. Other ranks of the nobility find their titles on the street map. Marquesses are represented by Bath Street, Bristol Road, Bute Street, Exeter Street, Hartington Place and Hartington Road, Lorne Road, and the man who gave his name to the rules of boxing is found at Queensbury Mews.

Earldoms were the inspiration for Burlington Street, Camden Street, Chatham Place, Chichester Place, Chichester Terrace, Chichester Drive West, Chichester Drive East, Clarendon Road, Coventry Street, Egremont Road, Essex Street, Guildford Road, Guildford Street, Jersey Street, Leicester Street, Mayo Road, Oxford Street, Powis Road, Powis Grove, and Shaftesbury Road.

Hereford Street, Sydney Street and Wentworth Street are all named after viscounts. While barons were the inspiration for Chesham Road, Chesham Street, Chesham Place, Holland Road, Southampton Street, Sudeley Street, Sudeley Place, Tichborne Street, Vernon Terrace, and Vernon Gardens.

Of course peers also have surnames in the usual sense. Making use of these has given Brighton several place names. Campbell Road is named for the dukes of Argyll. Both Cavendish Street and Cavendish Place point to the dukes of

Devonshire. The earls of Northampton are the Compton family, hence the naming of Compton Road and Compton Avenue.

As dukes of Buckingham the Grenville family are seen in Grenville Place, Grenville Street, Grenville Avenue, and Grenville Road. Grosvenor Street takes its name from the dukes of Westminster. Hervey Street can be traced to Ickworth House in Suffolk, home to the marquesses of Bristol. With their family seat at Arundel, the dukes of Norfolk gave a name to both Howard Road and Howard Place.

Lennox Street and Lennox Road can be traced back to Charles Lennox, an illegitimate son of Charles I. Montague Place and Montague Street probably point to Baron Montagu of Beaulieu, even though the places have acquired the extra letter. Both Pelham Street and Pelham Square are named for the earls of Chichester. Francis, the 5th Earl, played cricket for Sussex. The Russell family were dukes of Bedford and gave their name to Russell Square. Seymour Square and Seymour Street come from the family name of the dukes of Somerset. Stanley Road and Stanley Street are from the Stanleys; this family were created earls of Derby. The Wyndhams were earls of Egremont and gave their name to Wyndham Street.

Politicians are another favourite. Not only local officials but national and even international figures. British prime ministers are the most numerous, the following examples taking in no fewer than 18 terms of office. Arthur James Balfour took office in 1902, Balfour Road was named after him. Beaconsfield Road remembers Benjamin Disraeli, 1st Earl of Beaconsfield who was in office from 1874. Canning Street is after George Canning, in office for four months of 1827. Gladstone Place and Gladstone Road recall William Edward Gladstone, who first saw office in 1892 and is the oldest man ever to hold this position. In 1834 Viscount Melbourne took office, hence the name of Melbourne Street. Sir Robert Peel headed the government from 1846, hence Peel Road. John Russell, 1st Earl

Russell is seen in Russell Crescent. Sir Robert Walpole, who assumed the role in 1721, gave us Walpole Road. While the Duke of Wellington, albeit better remembered as a soldier, ran the country from 1828 and thus the names given to both Wellington Road and Wellington Street.

International figures are found in the form of presidents of the United States of America. Grant Street is after Ulysses S. Grant, who took office in 1869. Andrew Jackson, after whom Jackson Street is named, was president from 1829. Lincoln Street is named after Abraham Lincoln, who led the United States from 1861. Washington Street is after George Washington, the first holder of the office, inaugurated in 1789.

Local politicians have a head start when naming streets. However, to avoid controversy these are normally confined to those who serve as mayor who, while they do bring political ideas to the post, are trusted to act impartially and thus is only offered to those who are already well respected. Thus mayors of Brighton have given us Abbey Road, Aldrich Close, Beal Crescent, Blaker Street, Braybon Avenue, Brigden Street, Carden Avenue, Colbourne Road, Davey Drive, Ewart Street, Galliers Close, Hallett Road, Lucraft Road, Pankhurst Avenue, Sadler Way, Southall Avenue, Stringer Way, and Thompson Road.

Local landowners are an obvious source of street names, particularly as they are already associated with the land and thus avoids likely disputes. Here we find examples such as Curwen Place, Goldsmid Road, Harrington Road and Harrington Place, Mighell Street, Nevill Road and Nevill Avenue, Stanford Avenue and Stanford Road, Tidy Street, Western Road, and Whichelo Place.

Honorary freemen and women are also obvious subjects as their activities have already made them popular enough to earn the honour. Brighton further honoured them in naming Beatty Avenue, Carden Avenue, Churchill Square and Churchill Street, Haig Avenue, Saunders Park View and Saunders Park Rise, Stringer Way, and Wolseley Road.

With the roads developed shortly after the conflict, Boer War soldiers and the locations where fighting was most intense were in the news. Hence we find the names of Baden Road, Buller Road, Kimberley Road, Ladysmith Road, Mafeking Road, Milner Road, Natal Road, and Redvers Road.

An unusual idea for a number of streets are the names of philosophers and theologians, and other cerebral gentlemen. This gives Arnold Street, Baxter Street, Bentham Road, Carlyle Street and Carlyle Avenue, Cobden Road, Cromwell Street and Cromwell Road, Hampden Road, Howard Road and Howard Place, Luther Street, Lynton Street, and Milton Road.

Other place names are often chosen for street names, such as those here taken from the Isle of Wight such as Bembridge Street, Bonchurch Road, Brading Road, Carisbrooke Road, Sandown Road, Shanklin Road, Totland Road, and both Whippingham Road and Whippingham Street. The county of Kent proved the inspiration for Ashford Road, Dover Road, Hythe Road, and Sandgate Road. Even international place names have found their way to the sign at the end of the road. Canadian cities have given us Montreal Road, Toronto Terrace, and Quebec Street.

Important buildings have provided another dozen names. Abbeys are behind the names of Fountains Close, Hinton Close, Melrose Close, and Romsey Close. Castles have provided the names of Auckland Drive, Bamford Close, Bodiam Close, Durham Close, Hornby Road, Kenilworth Close, Knepp Close, Leybourne Road, Ludlow Rise, Norwich Close, Taunton Road, and Walmer Crescent.

Public houses include the Devil's Dyke Inn, situated in the valley with which it shares its name. Tradition tells this natural feature was an unfinished trench dug by Old Nick in an attempt to flood all the churches in the neighbourhood. The ancient road to Brighton from the valley is Dyke Road. It is crossed by Montpelier Road, another old route, which gave its name to the Montpelier. This is certainly not the original name but was coined when the area was developed.

It is the earliest known adoption of the French spa resort in England. Unfortunately this adoption resulted in the name being spelled with one 'L' instead of two. Named from the nearby river is the Cuckmere.

Location is also seen in the name of the Grand Central, alluding to the famous railway station in New York City, near Brighton's railway station. Similarly the Railway Bell is a pointer to the world's first electric all-Pulman service. Running from 1934 it was always referred to as the Brighton Belle, perhaps the pub should correct the spelling of 'Bell'.

While the Evening Star is a name given to the planet Venus, it was also the last steam locomotive built for British Rail. With the railway station only a minute or two's walk away, this does seem most appropriate. The Engineer is another railway name, it lies in the shadow of the viaduct, as does the Railway Hotel and the Station.

Queens Road gave its name to the Queens Head; Kensington Gardens to the Kensington; Rose Hill Tavern is on Rose Hill Terrace; Dyke Tavern is from its location on Dyke Road; the Prestonville Arms stretches the district name of Preston a little, both the Preston Park Tavern and the Park View are nearby; while the Stanmer Park Tavern overlooks Stanmer Park, with the Cleveland on Cleveland Road.

On County Oak Avenue we find the County Oak; Sutherland Road is the home of the Sutherland Arms; the Sudeley Arms in Sudeley Street; the Montague is in Montague Place; Rock Street has the Rock, while a more subtle link is seen in the Dragon being found in St George's Road. While the St James Tavern is on Madeira Place, it is a literal stone's throw from St James's Street.

Both the Racehorse and the Winner are pointers to Brighton Racecourse. The Park Crescent is on Park Crescent Terrace, the Race Hill is a reminder the course is at the summit. The Lectern reveals its location adjacent to the university, the name referring to the stand for notes in the lecture halls. The Newmarket Arms is officially on Bear Street but backs on to properties in Newmarket Street. The Foundry in Foundry Street probably points to where smelting once took place.

The Downs is a clear reference to the range of chalk hills which dominate the county. Saltdean gave its name to the Saltdean Tavern. The Montreal Arms is officially on Albion Hill, however, it stands at the apex of two converging side streets, Toronto Terrace and Montreal Road. Cobden Road is the location of the Cobden Arms; the Freshfield Inn is in Freshfield Road; the Market Tavern in Market Street; the Royal Pavillion found near the Royal Pavillion Tavern, and the most obvious of all is the Sussex public house.

The proximity of the ocean is reflected in pub names. Almost on the waterfront at the marina stands the West Quay, as is the case with both the Southcoast Tavern and the Beach public house. The Ship Inn and the Pilot are also 'marine' names, the latter being the individual who is responsible for bringing vessels into harbour through local knowledge of the seabed.

The Schooner Inn is not only a kind of ship but a glass used for sherry. Look along the quayside of almost any seaside place and you will see the pots and baskets which make the Basketmakers a relevant name here. The Smuggler may not have been the haunt of those bringing in contraband and yet the image of some, much as with that of the pirate, is now considered romantic.

The Geese Have Gone Over the Water is probably the longest pub name in Brighton, here the name was coined in 1988. The so-called Flight of the Earls remembers when Irish nobility, artists and poets left their homeland in droves fleeing English rule. The sign shows a sailing vessel departing Ireland for France.

Effectively the pub sign is an advertising board dating from the days when few could read and thus imagery was all important. These early signs were known as ale stakes, most often not a true stake but simply a tree stripped of its lower branches to which a sheaf of barley would be tied. Seeing this basic sign would

Brighton Sea Front.

tell travellers ale was brewed here. The product was also the basis for names such as the Hogshead, a large cask of varying volume used for wines and ales.

The Preston Brewery Tap gives the promise of draught beers. The Barley Mow refers to a major ingredient in the brewing process, the 'mow' being another word for a stack. The Mash Tun is the vat which contains the milled malt or grist; it is blended with a liquid to form a mash with the consistency of porridge. The Hop Poles marks those long poles forming the gridwork on which hops, a major brewing ingredient, were grown.

The Firkin Brewery use their name, that being a small cask, in all of their pub names. They also make it clear it is a pub name by linking it to another quite unrelated name while employing aliteration. All these criteria are answered by the Font and Firkin. While the Pull and Pump is an advertisement for the method of delivery: this is not a reference to an electrical dispenser but to hand-drawn ales.

If not advertising the product, names broadcast the warmth of the premises or the ambience of the inn itself or activities associated with the premises. One name we find here is the Jolly Brewer which advertises both the product and a good time found within. Similarly we find the Good Companions, a promise of a friendly welcome. The Hare and Hounds probably dates from the days when hare coursing was a popular sport before the advent of greyhound racing. The Cricketers shows a team played our national summer sport out of here.

The Fiddlers Elbow is an unusual name, one speaking of the constant movement of the musician drawing his bow across the strings of his chosen instrument. Several expressions have used these words to speak of something moving to and fro, back and forth or up and down. Hence if it is not a violinist, the most plausible explanation suggests the elbow belongs to the drinker who is enjoying his (or her) pint so much they feel compelled to take another drink.

Little doubt as to the message found at the Hikers Rest, the same message is seen in a different way at the Setting Sun where a drink is offered at the close of the day. At the Jury's Out a little refreshment is offered as the court is in recess while the jury deliberate a verdict. The Hand in Hand is a variation on an old friendly greeting. No Man Is An Island is a quote from a poem by John Donne, the message as a pub name offering a welcome, for we all need friends and colleagues. The Globe was an early and simple image showing all were catered for within.

It was not only Brighton's streets that were named for the upper classes who first made it the popular resort it is today. No name reflects the development of this place more than the Regency Tavern. There are a number of 'royal' pub names, none more obvious than the King and Queen. Known as the Sailor King, the William IV recalls the ruler of our nation for six days short of seven years from June 1830.

The Prince of Wales refers to the title held by the heir to the throne, rather than one specific holder. While the Royal Sovereign displays a fairly recent image of Queen Elizabeth II; these premises were built before she was born and almost certainly named after one of the many vessels of this name belonging to the Royal Navy. Both the Standard and the Royal Standard refer to the heraldic banner or flag which tells the story of the monarchy thus far and so changes with every new monarch.

The Prince Arthur is named after the Duke of Connaught and Strathearn, the third son of Queen Victoria, whose eldest child is marked by the Princess Victoria. The latter, Princess Victoria Adelaide Mary Louise, married the future German Emperor Frederick III in 1858, thus becoming German Empress and Queen of Prussia. Her brother Arthur is best remembered for his military career lasting some 40 years, the link to the county being through his title of Earl of Sussex.

When known as simply the George it would have been seen as a reference to St George, yet the real origin is seen in the modern name of the Prince George, this being the future George V. When Charles II hid in the branches of the oak tree at Boscobel in Shropshire it spawned a former public holiday and a host of pubs were named the Royal Oak. While the Queen's Arms shows support for the monarchy in general and the Queens Head was originally the same, the latter currently shows an image of the late Freddie Mercury. The Kings Arms was the local pub of choice of the Prince Regent, later George III, during his time in Brighton. The Victoria carries an image of a young Queen Victoria.

Other nobles are found such as the Duke of Norfolk, the family seat in Arundel. The Queensbury Arms is a reminder of the man who gave us the rules of boxing, the Queensbury Rules still a reminder how, no matter the circumstances, we are still gentlemen and a code of conduct should still be followed. This was the same Marquis of Queensbury whose libel case resulted in the imprisonment of Oscar Wilde.

The Compton Arms is from the family whose titles include Marquess of Wilmington and, very relevant here, Baron Wilmington. Famous as a soldier and for his final defeat of Napoleon, both the Duke of Wellington and the Wellington remember the man who also enjoyed a successful political career. The Marquess of Exeter features an old spelling of a rank of the nobility always given today as Marquis.

The Devonshire Arms is named for the Cavendish family, dukes of Devonshire. The Marlborough is from the dukes of Marlborough, the Churchill family whose seat is at Blenheim Palace. The Ranelagh is from the earldom created in the 17th century, taking the name of a part of Dublin. The Golden Lion is most often taken from the coat of arms of the Percy family, dukes of Northumberland. The Duke of Beaufort features the title held by the Somerset family. The marquess of Bath was the inspiration for the Bath Arms.

Religion might not seem the most obvious source for pub names today, however, when we consider the church was the second largest landholder in the country, and in rural situations these were the only two meeting places for most people, it does begin to make sense.

Horses have long been associated with pubs. From the earliest days when the landlord offered horses for hire and stabling if the traveller owned their own mount, through times when the innkeeper and the village blacksmith were the motorway services of their day; the huntsman and hounds, the coaching era, all are reflected in the names of pubs. The Horse and Groom is one example, the Waggon and Horses a reminder of how inns would act as agents in vast distribution networks before the coming of the canal and the later the railway. The Bugle is an inn named after the brass instrument blown to herald the arrival of the coach and horses, thus the equivalent of the modern bus stop.

Heraldry plays an important part in pub names. The Crescent began as an heraldic image of the moon, the real meaning uncertain as it depends whether the crescent was shown waxing or waning, or even lying on its back with 'horns' pointing upwards which indicates a family who fought on the Crusades to the Holy Land. The Eagle, the Spread Eagle, the Bear and the Stag are others, these powerful images found in far too many coats of arms to mention.

The Crown and Anchor features the badge found on the sleeve of Royal Navy petty officers, itself taken from the badge of the Lord High Admiral. The Black Horse has been chosen by many, including the 7th Dragoon Guards, a well-known high street bank, and the goldsmiths of London. However, in the case of the White Horse the image certainly represents the House of Hanover, the ruling house in Britain from 1714 to 1901.

Events have proved inspirational in the names such as the Battle of Trafalgar, fought on 21 October 1805. Trafalgar is a headland in Spain, northwest of the Straits of Gibraltar, with a name of Arabic origin in *tarf al-gharb* and meaning 'the cape of the west'.

Other places are a virtually endless source of inspiration for names, be they streets, houses, new estates or, in this case, pubs. The Walmer Castle and the

Dover Castle remind us of the fortifications built by Henry VIII, both of these examples found in Kent. Bevendean is a district name seen in the Bevendean Hotel, similarly the Hanover, the Hollingbury, and the Woodingdean are named for other places.

Many other individuals have suggested themselves as pub names. Robin Hood is one of the most popular figures in English history. Whether he existed or not is unimportant, it is the romance and the charisma associated with this figure which have led to its popularity as a pub name, especially in Sussex which is about as far from Sherwood Forest as it is possible to get. The earliest pubs of this name began as an image of a man dressed as a woodsman, soon seen in the famed Lincoln Green attire of the outlaws or Merrie Men of Sherwood Forest.

Few have had more pubs named after them than the Bard of Avon, here seen in the slightly different name of the Shakespeare's Head. In Southover Street we find the Sir Charles Napier, named after Admiral Sir Charles John Napier KCB GOTE RN. His 60 years' service in the Royal Navy saw action in the Napoleonic Wars, Syrian War, and the Crimean War.

While he does appear under different names, no individual has more pubs named after them than the man who commanded the British fleet at the Battle of Trafalgar. Here the name is seen as the Lord Nelson on Trafalgar Street and as Horatio's Bar on the pier. The unmistakeable image of his most famous vessel, HMS *Victory*, is seen on the sign outside the Victory Inn.

The image outside the Great Eastern is that of the great Victorian engineer Isambard Kingdom Brunel. This refers to SS *Great Eastern* which, when launched in 1858, was the largest vessel ever built until the *Mauretania* in 1907. Its launching was one of Brunel's few embrarrassing moments, for what was meant to be a quiet affair saw many thousands lining the banks of the Thames with three thousand tickets sold to enable some to watch from the shipyard itself. As the ship was much longer than the Thames was wide at this point, the vessel could not be launched lengthways in the traditional manner. Hence this massive bulk had to be sent down the slipway sideways, but the engineering problems for this kind of launch were new and untested. Thankfully Brunel was not present to see his latest project come to a halt on the slipway where it remained until launched successfully a few days later with a much smaller audience.

While the Franklin Tavern is not on Franklin Street, both are named after Benjamin Franklin, a founding father of the USA whose list of talents is quite amazing: author, printer, political theorist, politician, postmaster, scientist, musician, inventor, satirist, civic activist, statesman, and diplomat. Serving four terms as prime minister, and also giving his name to the Gladstone bag, William Gladstone is remembered by the Gladstone public house.

Local individuals have not only given their names to streets but have left their mark on the local pubs. Nearby Forest Row is held to have been the birthplace of William Caxton, he recalled by the Caxton Arms, and the man who is largely thought to have been the first to operate a printing press in England.

The Martha Gunn Inn was named in 1972, the winner of a competition organised by the brewery to rename the New Inn. Martha Gunn was a 'dipper', one who operated the bathing machines used by the women visiting Brighton beach to bathe. Styled as 'The Venerable Princess of the Bath' by the local press, this well-known figure appeared in many images including one where she is seen repelling the French with her mop. Martha was said to have been a close friend to the Prince of Wales, the future George IV, and had free reign of the royal households until her death in 1815.

Of course there are those names which do not fit into any category, such as the Lion and Lobster. Previously known as the Rockingham, this from the Marquess of Rockingham whose coat of arms does feature a lion on one side of the shield but a stag, not a lobster, on the other. In fact, the lobster is unknown in English heraldry. Hence this likely represents an advertisement for the seafood for which this establishment is rightly famous, while aliteration is always desirable.

The Sussex Yeoman is a difficult name for it depends upon the use of 'yeoman'. Of course our first thought is the Yeomen of the Guard, however, traditionally this described a farmer holding a small estate. There are examples of place names attached to 'Yeoman' all over the country, each depicts the name in its own way.

Once known as the New England, it is on the corner of New England Street, one pub has the almost unique name of the Cobbler's Thumb. With no suggestion of shoemaking in this area we must look elsewhere for potential meanings and but one phrase is found. Said to emanate from Ireland it is a rather unkind phrase, 'A face like a blind cobbler's thumb' describing someone rather ugly. Why this would suggest itself here is unclear for the place has an Australian, not an Irish, theme.

The Druids Arms marks a meeting place of the friendly society known as the Ancient Order of Druids. This group founded as early as 1781 are also found at the Druid's Head. It is impossible to give a meaning for the No Name Bar but etymology explains the development and here the pub with no name became such. The Pub With No Name has an identical origin.

The Spanish Lady has an odd evolution. Normally the bars would be named to compliment the pub but here quite the reverse, the Spanish theme coming after the naming of the Barcelona Bar and the Castile Saloon. The Albion Inn takes the Roman name for Britain, this being the Latin reference to the famous chalk cliffs of the south coast.

The Romans is a reminder of four centuries when Britain was a part of the Roman Empire. Once seen as an invasion, recently it is clear the Britons effectively 'applied for membership' in order to increase trade. The Brighton Rocks is undoubtedly a reference to this being a venue for music. Yet it also alludes to the 1938 novel by Graham Green, *Brighton Rock*, which has been adapted for the stage, radio, two films and even a musical.

Brightling

A name coming from a Saxon personal name and Old English *inga* and telling of the '(place of) the family or followers of a man called Beorhtel'. The name is recorded as Byrhtlingan in the early 11th century and as Brislinga in *Domesday*.

Darwell Hole has changed over the centuries, the original suffix to *deor* was not *wella* but *fald*. This name describes 'the hollow with a fold for deer or (more likely) animals'. That *deor* was the ancestor of the modern 'deer' is clear, however, it was also used as a generic term for animals. As these were said to be penned it would be logical to assume these were domesticated animals as, while not impossible, domesticated deer seems highly improbable.

Purchase Wood comes from a Saxon personal name and *ersc*, together giving 'the stubble field of a man called Puccel', the woodland later having the name transferred to here. Socknersh Manor was built in a region where the name shared the same suffix with the previous name. Here Middle English *soaken* precedes to speak of 'the wet stubble land'.

Broomhill

Looking at early records such as Prunhelle in the 12th century, Prumhelle in 1200, and Promhelle in 1195, it is clear the modern form is corrupted. The true origin is probably Old English *prume hyll* or 'the hill with plum trees'.

Bulverhythe

Found as Bulwareheda in the 12th century, the name is derived from Old English *burh ware hyth* and means 'the landing place of the dwellers in the town'. Here that town would have been nearby Hastings.

Burwash

Derived from Old English *burh ersc* and speaking of 'the ploughed land by the fortification'. This name is seen as Burhersce in the 12th century.

Crowhurst begins the local names. From Old English *crawe hyrst* or 'the wooded hill frequented by crows'. Frontridge is a corruption, understood to refer to 'the hill with a spring'. From *glede wisc* comes Glydwish, or 'the meadow frequented by kites'. These predatory birds were once a common sight in our skies. Goodsoal began as the Saxon personal name Guthhere followed by *holh* or 'corner of land'. This pattern is repeated in Turzes, although the suffix here is *ersc* and gives 'the stubble field of a man called Tirheard'.

Pubs here include the Kicking Donkey, a name referring to the product and to the times when most prospective customers worked the land and only came to the village proper once a week. Clearly this was not good for business and thus, as own-brews were the norm, the product was taken to the customers. This name tells of the small casks delivered to nearby farms using a small cart pulled by a donkey.

Others found here are the Rose and Crown, a patriotic name with the rose representing the nation and the crown its monarch. The Bell Inn shows a link to the church, many early inns were built on church land as the monks were brewing the ale. Finally there is the Wheel with its sign showing this inn worked, not with a blacksmith, but a wheelwright.

At Burwash is a grand mansion called Bateman's. For half of his adult life this was home to Rudyard Kipling, who used this area as the setting for his stories *Puck of Pook's Hill*, published in 1906, and *Rewards and Fairies*, published in 1910. The village war memorial includes the name of Kipling, not the writer but his son, Jack, a casualty of World War One.

Buxted

Found as Boxted in 1199, the meaning of this Old English place name depends whether the origin is *boc stede* and 'the place of the beech trees' or *box stede* 'the place where box trees grow'.

What began as Bevingworth is today seen in the name of Bevingford. The present ending self-explanatory, the name began in a Saxon personal name with

Buxted village sign.

Eleventh-century church of St Margaret the Queen in Buxted Park.

St Margaret the Queen Church's altar.

Old English *inga worth* or 'the enclosure of the family or followers of a man called Beofa'. Etchingwood has many similarities; it also began with a Saxon name and *inga worth* and thereafter transferred, although here to a woodland. Beginning as Etchingworth, this speaks of 'the enclosure of the family or followers of a man called Haecca'.

Other names found here include Hendall, from *hind dael* or 'the valley frequented by hinds'. Shadwell takes its name from 'the shallow spring or stream'. While the name of Totease dates from the days when it was said to be 'the area of brushwood of a man called Totta'.

To refer to the local as the Buxted Arms seems pointless, for the locals would be well aware of where it was. However, the real targets are visitors and travellers, named in the hope it would be remembered before others such as the White Hart here. While the white male deer was first seen as a pub name following the coronation of Richard II, very soon afterwards it became the generic term for all pubs.

Heading south-east is Nan Tuck's Lane, a name which dates back to the early 19th century and recalls a resident who murdered her husband in 1810 with a massive dose of poison. Her crime quickly became public knowledge and the hunt for her was on. Her local knowledge saw her evade them until it became clear she was seeking the sanctity of the church. She soon realised she could never outrun them in this straight race and so, nearing exhaustion, detoured into the woods. Her body was never found although since that time her ghost has been reported along the lane which is now named after her. Back in the woods a patch of land is said to have been her final resting place. This perfectly circular area is completely infertile and no vegetation has ever been seen growing here.

Camber

Found as Camere in 1375, Portus Camera in 1397, and as Caumbre in 1442. The basic name is derived from Old French *cambre* which refers to 'a room, an enclosed place'. This is clearly not an actual room, nor indeed a building of any kind but a reference to a natural feature. However, to find that feature we must examine maps from yesteryear, one of which shows an area probably used as a harbour. Today the estuary of the River Rother has silted up.

Public houses begin with the Green Owl which, as with any oddly-coloured animal, suggests it is heraldic. While the owl is well represented in heraldry, where it always stands in profile but faces fully forward, invariably this can be traced to a French or Norman family, although no example suggests itself.

It is a very different story when it comes to the Camber Castle, the shell of which still stands on the route between Winchelsea and Rye. The Royal William is doubtless a reference to King William VI, the so-called Sailor King whose reign ended in 1837. Camber Castle was one of 30 of Henry VIII's so-called Device Forts also referred to as Henrican Castles. It began as a circular tower constructed by Sir Edward Guldeford in 1514, it was then incorporated into the new fort completed 30 years later. With the silting up of the river it made the castle obsolete and in 1637 the place was abandoned.

Catsfield

Here is a name listed as Cedesfeld in *Domesday* and as Cattesfeld in the 12th century. Together these suggest two possible origins: if this is Old English *catt feld* it would give 'the open land frequented by wild cats', or perhaps the first element is a Saxon personal name and thus 'the open land of a man called Catt'.

Fatland is derived from Old English *fyrhthe lands*, 'the agricultural lands by the woodland scrub'. Freckley Wood adds *leah* to a Saxon personal name to describe 'the woodland clearing of a man calld Fricca'.

The White Hart became popular soon after the coronation of Richard II in 1377, it being a part of the King's coat of arms. However, his reign began when he was still a minor and ended when he was deposed and eventually killed at Pontefract Castle, so he can hardly be the reason this name has remained very popular over the intervening centuries. That it is still used is entirely down to the phrase of White Hart being used as a generic term for all public houses, much as the Hoover is used to refer to vacuum cleaners today.

Chailey

Listed as Cheagle in the 11th century, this comes from Old English *ceacga leah* and describes 'the woodland clearing where gorse grows'.

Beven Bridge tells us the place was known as 'the corner of land of a man called Beofa' before the bridge was constructed. Lovel Barn comes from *hlot* or 'the land divided into lots'. Warningore Farm adds *inga ora* to a Saxon personal name to tell of 'the bank of land of the family or followers of a man called Waenna'. Slabcastle is a derogatory term, a reference to a small house roofed with the local Horsham slate. Waspbourne Farm shows this was once 'the stream by the bridal paths', a charming picture of Saxon life painted simply by defining the name.

The Horns Lodge public house has certainly been on this site for two centuries, although there is good reason to believe it is at least 50 years older. The name refers to this being the cottages on the edge of the estate, whose family will have featured the stags' horns in their arms. Such a device is found for families whose ancestry is European, particularly Norman. While there was a family named Norman here in the 18th century, this is rather late to be considered as the origin. At the Kings Head the name shows support for the monarchy.

Once there were two other pubs, the Swan House and the Five Bells. Yet at this time there were five churches, St Peter's, St Martin's, Chailey Free Church, St John's, and St Mary's, meaning there were more churches than pubs!

Chalvington

A 'farmstead associated with a man called Cealfa'; this name comes from Old English *ing tun* and a Saxon personal name and appears as Calvintone in *Domesday*.

Lover's Farm may sound romantic, and there is no reason to doubt John and Margery Loverd had a deep and meaningful relationship. However, it was their surname which gave this place name; they were first recorded here in 1521.

Chiddingly

Found as Cetelingei in *Domesday* and as Chittingeleghe in the early 13th century, this is probably a Saxon personal name and Old English *inga leah* describing 'the woodland clearing of the family or followers of a man called Citta'.

It is not difficult to see Nash Street as coming from *atten ash*, meaning 'at the ash trees'. Note the final letter of *atten* has migrated to the front of *ash* to become Nash, a common occurence when the following word begins with a vowel and due to a misunderstanding of the pronunciation. Honeywick Wood is the present version of the place name which began as 'the farm where honey is produced'. Honey, a valued natural product, was used extensively in Saxon cuisine as sugar was not available and the word is still recognised. Here the suffix is *wic*, normally seen as 'dairy farm' but correctly should be given as 'specialised farm'; clearly the speciality is the production of honey.

Chiltington, East

One of two places in Sussex so named, hence the addition. This example is first seen in 1086, the *Domesday* record of Childetune showing this is probably a Celtic hill name with Old English *ing tun* and 'the farmstead associated with the slope of the Cilte'. However, it may be that the first element represents a district name Ciltine, itself derived from the hill name which has yet to be defined.

Wootton Farm comes from *wudu tun* 'the farmstead of or near the wood'. Yokehurst would normally be said to come from Old English *geoc hyrst*, however, this would mean 'helping wooded hill' but that makes no sense. Here the modern form is 'yoke', which shares a common root with *geoc* for the yoke across the oxen helped the animal pull the plough or cart. Therefore we can deduce that while the suffix is unchanged, the former has taken on a related word but a very different meaning. The wooded hill is growing with hornbeam, the tree providing the raw material for the production of yokes.

The pub sign outside the Jolly Sportsman sends two messages. Its original name was Sportsman, showing games were played within and/or outdoor sports organised here. Jolly being added much later to suggest those playing games were happier here.

Coleman's Hatch

Here is 'the forest gate associated with the Coleman family', where Old English *haecc* follows the lords of the manor who were certainly here by the 13th century. The name is found in 1495 as Colmanhacche.

Crowborough

Listed as Cranbergh in 1292, this is from *crawe beorg*, Old English for 'the mound frequented by crows'.

Pub names include the Wheatsheaf, which became a pub name following its use as a device in the coat of arms of both the Brewers' Company and the Worshipful Company of Bakers. The latter is by far the most numerous, the landlord often doubling as the baker and wanting to advertise. The Crow and Gate features a sign where two five-bar gates represent the wings on a crow. In reality the name probably represents the opposite, a typical rural scene where two crows are sitting on a single gate.

Taking local place names, both of obvious meaning, are the Crowborough Cross and the Whitehill Tavern. In the case of the Coopers Arms in Coopers Lane both probably share an origin indicating a maker of barrels, casks and tubs. In the plough the landlord offers a welcome to all who work the land which, when the name was first popular, meant just about everyone. In later times alternatives appeared and here the Plough and Horses is a quite rare example. Note the horse did not pull a plough until comparatively recently, for most of its days the plough was drawn by oxen. There was a period when both were used, the horse in the lead for an increase in speed and the oxen behind for great power at slower speeds – effectively two gears!

Speaking both of the product and the promise of the mood within, is the possibly unique name of the High Spirits. A clear invitation is offered by the delightfully-named Welcome Stranger. It is certain the Half Moon Inn has an heraldic origin, however, the sign depicts a full moon, making its beginning difficult to understand. Note that at a full moon, indeed at any time, half of the moon is illuminated by the sun. The White Hart began as an heraldic image with the accession of Richard II in 1377, however, thereafter it became a generic term for all public houses.

Crowhurst

Records of this name begin in 772 as Croghyrste and later seen as Croherst in 1086. This is Old English *croh hyrst* and 'the wooded hill near the corner of land'.

Cuckmere, River

Listed as Cokemere Bay in 1352 and as Cookemere in 1335, this name describes the '*mere* or pool of a man called Cuca'.

D

Dallington

Seen as Dalintone in the *Domesday* survey of 1086, this comes from a Saxon personal name and Old English *ing tun* and telling of 'the farmstead of a man called Dalla'. Dallington Forest was named from this place.

Danehill

Listed as Denne in 1279 and as Denhill in 1437, this is from Old English *denn hyll* and describes 'the hill by the woodland pasture'. The hamlet of Chelworth, once an independent settlement, began life as 'the *worth* or enclosure of a man called Ceola'.

Denton

The earliest surviving record of this name is exactly the same as the modern form and found as such in the ninth century. Here from Old English *denu tun* comes 'the farmstead in the valley'.

Dicker (Upper & Lower)

Two place names with a single origin in Middle English *dyker* meaning 'ten', probably a reference to the rent figure. The first record of this name is as Diker in 1229, the additions coming much later and requiring no explanation.

As a pub name the Plough has been among the most popular in the land since at least the 16th century. At this time most scraped a living directly from the land, hence a welcome is offered to one and all. Imagery is all-important in pub signs, indeed they exist solely because most were illiterate. As the image of the horse-drawn plough is still instantly recognised, an actual plough or a representation of same, would have been used in place of a painted sign. It is more durable if an old example can be obtained; it is certainly cheaper and, as that found on the bay of the Plough at Upper Dicker shows, a most pleasing alternative.

Ditchling

Records of this name include Dicelinga in 765 and as Dicelinges in 1086. Here the Saxon personal name is followed by Old English *inga* and refers to the '(place of) the family or followers of a man called Dicel'.

Frag Barrow is a badly corrupted Old English *fryth* meaning 'wooded hill'. Piddingworth features a Saxon personal name with *inga worth* or 'the enclosure of the family or followers of a man called Pydel'.

There are two pub names here, both appearing to be symbolic. That is certainly the case with the White Horse, representing the House of Hanover who ruled here from 1714 to 1901 and included the longest reigning king, George III, and the longest reigning queen, Victoria. With the Bull the imagery is less certain, such a powerful image has been chosen by many families and organisations, yet here the name lacks a colour which would confirm this origin. However, it may still be a representation, this image appears on the seal of the pope's edicts which is why such are referred to as papal bulls. Of course, we cannot entirely rule out this simply being a favourite animal.

E

Eastbourne

A name first seen in *Domesday* as simply Burne. This basic name is derived from Old English *burna* meaning 'spring or stream'. Not until 1310 do we find Estbourne, the self-explanatory addition distinguishing it from Westbourne.

Street names include Denton Road, a family name which can be traced back to the 13th century when one Lescelina de Denton was in residence. Greys Road remembers the family of Richard Grey, he being listed in a document dated 1490. Allfrey Road remembers a family who were resident here.

Angus Close and Wedderburn Road were both named after Angus Wedderburn. The Attfield family farmed Winkney Farm, hence the name of Attfield Walk. Former lord of the manor Bartholomew Badlesmoe, here from 1308, is recalled by Badlesmoe Road. The land on which Bernard Lane was cut was owned by the Metropolitan Railway Estates Co., this being named after the chairman Sir Bernard Docker.

Bradford Street remembers an important family in Eastbourne from the 17th century. Brodie Place took the name of Alexander Brodie, vicar of

Eastbourne for 10 years from 1810. Chatfield Crescent took the name of the family who lived and worked on the land which was formerly a part of Spots Farm. Coltstocks Farm was on land now occupied by Coltstocks Road.

There really was a duck decoy at what is now called Decoy Drive. The Eastbourne Corporation Motor Omnibus Department garage occupied land where Ecmod Road is found today. Hammond Drive commemorates the general manager of the Eastbourne Gas Co., S.W. Hammond. Laleham Girls School was on the land where Laleham Close was cut.

Leeds Road was named to remember the workers from that city who were employed on the site of the World War One airfield. Similarly Oldcamp Road marks the site of the World War One Military Convalescent Camp known as Summerdown.

The Dukes of Devonshire, major landholders in every part of the country, are seen in Cavendish Place, the family name, and Chatsworth Gardens, the seat of the dukedom. Cobbold Avenue recalls Lieutenant Colonel I. Cobbold, who married Lady Blanche Cavendish.

Calverley Road is named after former resident Miss Cordelia Calverley. From 1339 the de Roos family were lords of this manor for some two centuries, hence the name of De Roos Road. Filder Close was named from the family of tenant farmers. Bookseller Gilbert Foyle gave his name to Foyle Way.

Glynde Avenue was where the Brand family resided at Glynde House. Gorringe Road recalls the family who held this land from 1818. Hurst Road was named for the Hurst family, associated with the town from the 19th century. Motcombe Farm, itself named from Roger de Motcombe here in the early 13th century, is remembered by Motcombe Lane.

Roseveare Road honours the name of Major Leslie Roseveare, who worked as Borough Surveyor (1920–39). Susans Road is on the land once known as Susans Farm. Star Road took the name of the Star Inn. Sydney Tugwell worked

Eastbourne's famous pier.

Winckney Farm and is recalled by Tugwell Road, the farm appears at the end of Winckney Road. Weatherby Close is named after the resident family.

Developers are remembered in street names. Albert Parade was built by Albert E. Hill. During the 1930s Benjamin Groves developed the area around Benjamin Close. Fennells Close remembers Robert Fennell, local benefactor. Similarly Yielding's Close recalls another, John Yielding.

Politicians are always a favourite for new developments, and not just in more recent times. Brand Road recalls Sir Henry Brand, Speaker of the House of Commons 1872–84. Former mayor of Eastbourne John Collier gave his name to Collier Close. Alderman George Homewood gave his name to Homewood Close. Alderman A.J. Marshall served (1913–67) and is recalled by Marshall Road.

Crumbles Pond is a very minor feature in a name meaning 'the small fragment of land'. Moatcroft Road was a smallholding, hence the 'croft', before becoming the site of a Norman manor house, hence the 'moat'. Ocklynge occupies the 'ridge of land where oak trees grow'. Tutts Barn was associated with John Tut in 1332, while later, in 1485, the family of William Whytbred was living near Whitebread Hole. Constructed as part of the defences against the very real threat of invasion by Napoleonic forces, the martello towers remain a symbol of the nation's defences. The local example is known as Wish Tower, its name derived from the 'meadow' on which it was constructed, in Old English known as a *wisc*.

Public houses of Eastbourne fall into most of the usual categories. Advertising location is all-important, for there is no point having the best beers or the most salubrious premises if nobody knows where to find it. The Mill is a modern building on an old site alongside the river. On Star Road we find the Star Inn, itself possibly an indication this is on church land for this symbolises the Virgin Mary and a church dedicated to St Mary the Virgin is found fewer than 200 yards away. However, we cannot ignore the Star Brewery, based in Eastbourne, although all three would most likely share a common origin.

The Drive is on Victoria Drive, the Crown is on Crown Street, the Kingfisher Tavern stands on Kingfisher Drive, and the Friday Street Farm is on Farm Street. An Eastbourne postcode of BN21 is a modern version of a location name, a brand new name compared to the Gildredge which is coming from Gildredge Park and Gildredge Manor, home to a family of that name since the 16th century and who owned much of Eastbourne. In the case of the Chelsea Corner the place does stand on a corner in a region known as Little Chelsea.

Terminus Street leads to the railway station, also reminding us the line terminates here, and was named at the same time as the Terminus Hotel. The 16th century building which is now home to the Counting House was once where a local business had the accounting office. The stream which gave us the latter part of Eastbourne is also the basis for the Bourne public house. The Parkfield is not on Parkfield Terrace but just a literal stone's throw away, itself named for running alongside Hampden Park.

A coastal location is seen in the naming of the Ship and also the Shore. Similarly the Pilot Inn is named after the man charged with navigating the tricky waters of a harbour, the term in use at sea well before it was applied to an airman. The Beach, the Marine, and the Ocean Wave are all pointers to the coast.

Less obvious is the Royal Sovereign, named after the lighthouse vessel which warned of the danger of the shoal (it also taking the name of Royal Sovereign Shoal) since 1875. In 1971 a concrete tower replaced the vessel and also took the name of Royal Sovereign. From a porthole on board a ship there is a view of the ocean, the same can be seen through the windows of the bars at the Porthole.

Normally seen as a royal reference, yet if we take the image outside the Windsor Tavern as the real origin, this dates from before the House of Windsor's existence. The sign shows a sailing ship, a square-rigged bark (or barque). Perhaps this is the vessel fitting this description and named *Windsor* which rescued the crew of the *Champion* off the Cape Horn on 3 January 1877.

The Redoubt Fortress at Eastbourne houses a military museum.

The Seven Sisters is on Seven Sisters Road, both names found elsewhere in England where they refer to the Pleiades, an open star cluster which is the most obvious to the naked eye. However, the Eastbourne version is a reference to the chalk cliffs. These coastal features are the remnants of dry valleys which continue to be eroded by the English Channel. Each of seven valleys are named, and an eighth hill has been created by the erosion. In order (west to east) these are Haven Brow, Short Bottom, Short Brow, Limekiln Bottom, Rough Brow, Rough Bottom, Brass Point, Gap Bottom, Flagstaff Point, Flagstaff Bottom, Flat Hill, Flathill Bottom, Baily's Hill, Michel Dean, and Went Hill Brow. These take those following the South Downs Way along an undulating course.

Taking its name from the range of forts built along the southern coast is the Martello Inn. This line of defences amounted to some 70 towers along the coast offering views towards the Continent in the hope of preventing enemy landings, particularly those under the command of Napoleon Bonaparte. Their design is based upon that found by the English fleet when they captured Corsica and Cape Mortella, a name they attempted to copy but managed to get slightly wrong.

If not advertising, then what is on offer seems the sensible explanation, although to some degree both are promoted by the Cellar Bar and Restaurant. Both beers and wines come in a variety of casks and barrels of many sizes. Among these is the container which has given a name to the Hogshead, a large cask of indeterminate capacity.

Offering a welcome is always a good idea, the Dewdrop Inn a phonetic invitation to please 'do drop in'. Much less obvious is the Bibendum, from a source which would be highly obscure to the majority. It can be traced back to the first century BC when the poet Horace wrote an ode recording Octavian's victory over Antony and Cleopatra. Here we find the Latin phrase *Nunc est*

The Crown and Anchor at Eastbourne.

The iconic image of Eastbourne's Marine Parade.

bibendum meaning 'now is the time to drink' used in the sense of 'celebration'.

Heraldry and symbolism forms the basis for many pub names. The Crown and Anchor features the badge of the Lord High Admiral, also seen on the arm badge of the Royal Navy's petty officers. The Eagle is more difficult to tie down to one coat of arms. This powerful image has been chosen by many, from landholding families to nations and empires such as the USA, Russia and the Roman Empire. Similarly the Black Horse also represents many families, also a well-known bank, the goldsmiths of Lombard Street in London, and the 7th Dragoon Guards.

The Dolphin is a common pub name with numerous sources. Once it was a much more common surname, there have been numerous ships named after a creature always seen as the sailors' friend. However, here the image is heraldic, representing either the Fishmongers Company or the Company of Watermen and Lightermen.

To name a pub the Black Sheep is to suggest one who fails to fit in and seems unlikely, for while pub names suggesting something different is commonplace, this phrase is always used in a negative sense. Thus this is heraldic and a device we know will have come from a European (possibly Norman) coat of arms for only the Ram and Lamb are found in British heraldry.

Possibly the most numerous group are the 'royal' pub names. The Alexandra Arms recalls Queen Alexandra of Denmark, consort of Edward VII. Prince Albert takes another consort, this time the husband of Queen Victoria and father-in-law of Queen Alexandra. His wife was the inspiration for the Victoria Hotel. The Kings Arms is a more general show of support for the crown.

Other nobles are seen in the shape of the Hartington, both it and Hartington Place taking a title of the Duke of Devonshire, also Marquess of Hartington. His wife was the daughter of Richard Boyle, his title giving a name to the Earl of Burlington. The Arlington Arms recalls the barons Arlington. The Waverley

View of Eastbourne from Warren Hill, Eastbourne Downland.

comes from Viscount Waverley of Westdean, the title held by Sir John Anderson, a line created in the 17th century. As a statesman he served as Governor of Bengal, Member of Parliament, Lord Privy Seal, Home Secretary, Lord President of the Council, and Chancellor of the Exchequer.

Not specific individuals but romantic imagery are seen in two names. In the case of the Cavalier the royal connection is to the 17th century Royalists who fought on the side of Charles I in the English Civil War. Cavaliers, often described as 'Gay Cavaliers', is used in the sense to describe a flamboyant, joyful and heroic figure. Similarly the Buccaneer paints a romantic image, while the synonym 'pirate' would be seen as a blood-thirsty villain.

Locals who are remembered include the prominent Hurst family. Former residents of Ocklynge Manor, this family of brewers and millers gave their name to the Hurst Arms. The history of public houses has been associated with horses until the last hundred years or so. While the Tally Ho instantly brings to mind the cry which went up by the huntsman when their quarry was spotted, this is

No doubting the direction of the prevailing wind at Warren Hill, Eastbourne Downland.

not the equine connection here. Here the Tally Ho refers to the name of a famous stagecoach which stopped at Eastbourne. Religion is the basis for the Lamb Inn, Christ also known as the 'lamb of God'.

While among those which do not fit into any category is the New Inn, which is a common name clearly stating this was not the first pub here. Probably this would be better named as the 'newer' inn. The Greenhouse is neither that colour nor does it have a great deal of glass. It does not seem to be a reference to an overly eco-friendly establishment either, indeed the name seems to have been created solely to show a relationship between here and its sister the Beachhouse, the latter leaving no doubt as to its location. The Pubb is a modern name, the misspelling deliberate as it is eye-catching.

Eastdean

From Old English *east denu* comes a name listed as Esdene in *Domesday*. Here the name tells us this place was 'the eastern valley', that is relative to Westdean.

What began as 'the valley of a man called Maegla' is today seen as Malecomb. Selhurst is from *sele ersc* 'the wooded hill with or by a building'. The twin names of Open Winkins and Closed Winkins share the element *wince* meaning 'corner place', the additions are self-explanatory. Birling Farm comes from *ing* with a Saxon personal name describing 'the place associated with a man called Baera'.

At the Tiger Inn the sign points to a 19th-century origin in the striped attire of black boys who were employed in the household of the rich. Not really servants but a fashion accessory, they were most often seen in stripes of black and yellow.

Eridge Green

Seen as Ernerigg in 1202, here 'the ridge frequented by eagles' comes from Old English *earn hrycg*.

Etchingham

Found as Hechingeham in 1158, here a Saxon personal name and Old English *inga ham* combine to tell us it was 'the homestead of the family or followers of a man called Ecci'. The name is almost certainly indicating that Ecci was not living here, indeed he probably never did but was named posthumously.

Bellhurst started life as an independent settlement known as 'the *hyrst* or wooded hill of a man called Bella'. Another personal name gave us Kitchingham, here suffixed by *inga ham* it speaks of 'the homestead of the family or followers of a man called Cycci'.

Pub names begin with the Bear Inn, where the lack of a colour, black, brown, white, etc., would suggest this is probably not heraldic. Hence this would likely show a place where the former 'sport' of bear-baiting was held. This involved tethering the bear to a post and dogs were encouraged to attack the unfortunate creature. Sadly this remained perfectly legal in England until as recently as 1835. A third suggestion source should also be mentioned, however, it does seem unlikely the landlord would tolerate the spelling of 'bear' instead of 'beer' for very long.

The White Horse is heraldic, a reference to the House of Hanover, rulers in Britain between 1714 and 1901. While the Cross Keys Inn features an image taken from the arms of St Peter, this is not the present dedication of the church at Etchingham.

Names which have a connection with this village include Henry Corbould, who is buried here. Not a name which instantly springs to mind but everyone will have seen his work for he was the man who designed the first postage stamp, the famed Penny Black, which became the basis for every subsequent stamp.

Haremere Hall was home to James Temple during the 1620s, although it was not for another 30 years that he achieved lasting notoriety. A puritan, he fought at the Battle of Edgehill, supported Parliament against the King, and eventually became MP for Bramber in 1645. In 1649 he was appointed a judge in the trial of Charles I of England and was the 28th of the 59 signatures of the King's death warrant. In 1660 at the Restoration of the Monarchy in the form of Charles II he was charged with regicide. Despite being guilty he managed to avoid execution but was sent Jersey where he was imprisoned until the day he died.

Ewhurst

Records of this name include Weste in 1086, as Hyerst in 1195, as Hiuherst in 1202, and as Houehurst in 1223. This comes from Old English *iw hyrst* and describes 'the yew tree hill'.

Examples of local names all begin with a Saxon personal name, each having different Old English suffixes. Badland Shaw features *land* and tells of 'the agricultural land of a man called Bada', with the later addition of *sceaga* 'small wood, copse'. Lordine Court occupies an area which already had the name of 'the *staeth* or landing place of a man called Leofred'. In the case of Udiham there is a second Old English element, thus *ing ham* gives us 'the homestead associated with a man called Huda'. Lastly Yorkshire Wood, nothing to do with the county but a corruption of 'the buildings of a man called Eorcon'.

Fairlight

The earliest record of this place name dates from around the end of the 12th century. Here, from Old English *fearn leah*, comes 'the woodland clearing where ferns grow'. This name was later transferred to Fairlight Cove which, in turn, gave a name to the local pub, the Cove.

Local names include Covehurst Bay, which dates from Saxon times when there was 'a cove marked by a wooded hill'. Frostbourne has no connection with icy temperatures, this is a corruption of *frogga burna* 'the stream known for its frogs'. Stonelink is located, as the name tells us, on 'the stony slope'.

Falmer

Seen as Falemere in 1086, this name comes from Old English *fealu mere* and describes 'the fallow coloured pool'.

Here we find the similarly named Balmer, this describing 'the pool by the *burh* or fortified place'. Bevendean began life as 'the *denu* or valley of a man called Beofa'. Moustone comes from 'the stone of a man called Mul'. Patchway was known as 'the way of a man called Paeccel'.

The Swan Inn features the majestic bird seen all over England. Such an image made for a fine sign and equally an excellent device in any coat of arms, it representing the Vintners' Company, the Poulters' Company, the Musicians' Company, the earls of Essex, and King Edward III.

Firle, West

The addition may be self-explanatory but the meaning of the basic name would be difficult to recognise today. It comes from Old English *fierel* or 'the place where oak trees grow', the name recorded as simply Ferle in *Domesday*.

Adder Wells has nothing to do with snakes, this is a corruption of 'the spring marked by apple trees'. Charleston is certainly from *ceorl lac tun*, although whether this should be seen as 'the farmstead of the freemen or peasant by the stream' or, with the first element used as a personal name, 'the farmstead by the stream of a man called Ceorl'. What began as 'the hill of a man called Crotta' is seen as Crotteburgh on modern maps. Lastly Newelm, from *atten wielle* meaning 'at the spring or stream' where the last part of the first element has migrated to become part of the second.

The local is the Ram Inn, an indication this pub was associated with the wool trade early on in its 500 year history. Several coats of arms have taken the ram as a device, in use since the 14th century.

Fletching

Domesday records this as Flescinges, later seen as Fletchingh in 1202, and as Flecchinghe in 1268. Here from a Saxon personal name and Old English *inga* is the '(place) of the family or followers of a man called Flecci'.

Local names begin with Barkham, early forms showing this began as *birce ham* or 'the homestead by a birch tree'. Pilt Down, a name synonymous with one of the greatest archaeological hoaxes, began life as 'the hill of a man called

Pileca'. Ruttingham gets its name from *inga hamm* and a personal name to speak of 'the hemmed-in land of the family or followers of a man called Rota'. Sheffield Park was *sceap feld* 'the open land where sheep are reared'. While Woolpack Farm is a real wolf in sheep's clothing as this is from *wulf pytt* or 'the pit frequented by wolves'.

Flitteridge Wood comes from *flit hrycg* or 'the ridge of dispute', clearly somewhere the boundaries and ownership were not simply disputed but one where such went on for a considerable time in order for it to become a place name. However, the final minor name of Clapwater is that which delights the author most of all. Here we have a name which, simply by defining the meaning, paints a picture from history which no painter could ever have reproduced and no camera could ever capture. The 'clap' here is that of the hoppers on the mill wheel as they hit the surface of the water. Thus not only do we have a mental image of this scene but also a soundtrack to animate it and bring it to life.

Symbolism has given us the names of both pubs in Fletching. The Rose and Crown shows this to be a patriotic establishment, the rose is representative of the nation and the crown its monarchy. Heraldry is certainly the origin with the Griffin Inn, as the animal is mythological and rarely seen outside of coats of arms. However, whose coat of arms is very difficult to discover for it has been adopted by so many families and no wonder, when it is the supposed result of crossing the king of beasts, the lion, with the most powerful bird, the eagle.

Folkington

Early records of this name include that of Fochintone in *Domesday* and as Folkintone in the middle of the 12th century. Here the Saxon personal name and Old English *ing tun* combine to tell of 'the farmstead associated with a man called Folca'.

Locally we find The Links, not a reference to golf but from Old English *hlinc* in a plural form meaning 'ridges, terraces, ledges'. Nata Wood has two equally plausible origins. either from a personal name and 'the wood of a man called Nata' or from *neata wudu* 'the wood near where cattle were reared'.

Forest Row

Listed as Forstrowe in 1467, here Middle English *forest row* tell of 'the row in Ashdown Forest'. This could have been a row of trees or cottages, while the forest name is discussed under its own entry.

Brambletye speaks of 'the enclosure marked by brambles'. It is surprising to find this Middle English suffix virtually unchanged in modern times, it is still seen in the name of the Brambletye Hotel. Cansiron is another name which has developed somewhat unusually from its beginnings of 'the corner of land frequented by herons or cranes', normally we would have expected this to have become Cranhall.

Forest Row is twinned with the French town of Milly-la-Foret.

Plawhatch Hall is derived from *plega hatch*, telling us there was a path here 'leading to the place of play' and clearly where sporting events and games took place fairly frequently. From a Saxon personal name with Old English *inga hrycg*, Dallinridge Farm describes 'the ridge of land of the family or followers of a man called Daedel', the element *inga* also revealing the named individual was not living here, indeed the place was named posthumously.

We should expect to find the Foresters Arms as the first pub in Forest Row. In the case of the Swan the name is almost certainly a reference to the waterbird, although an heraldic image cannot be ruled out entirely. Chequers can be traced back to Roman times when it was seen outside an inn where a board game was played within. Later the same chequerboard image was used to represent a moneyer, the word still seen in the title of the man who runs the nation's finances, the Chancellor of the Exchequer.

The subject of money was on everyone's lips following an event here on 27 June 1801. A mail coach climbed Wall Hill but was held up by John Beatson and his adopted son William Whalley Beatson who had been hiding in a meadow at the foot of the hill and had followed the ascent, bringing them to a halt at the top around the strike of midnight. The robbery was thought to have brought them between four and five thousand pounds. When they were brought to trial in March 1802 Judge Baron Hotham sentenced them to death by hanging. Appropriately the gallows were erected on the spot where the robbery took place and both men were executed for their crime on 17 April 1802. A crowd of more than 3,000 were present.

Framfield

A name listed as Framelle in 1086 and as Fremefeld in 1257, here a Saxon personal name and Old English *feld* speak of 'the open land of a man called Fremma or Fremi'.

Here we find Crockstead, a name telling us this was 'the place where pots are made'. Peckham Farm is from Old English describing 'the homestead on a peak'. The same tongue is seen as the origin of Tickerage Wood, from *ticcen hrycg* or 'the ridge where young goats are reared'.

The Hare and Hounds is a reminder of hare coursing, a sport banned in 2005 in the UK. As a sport it was a test of the ability of the dogs and their owner to chase, overtake and turn the hare rather than catching the target.

Frant

Here a single Old English element, *fiernthe*, refers to 'the place overgrown with fern branches'. The earliest record dates from 956 where it is seen as Fyrnthan.

Bayham Abbey was constructed on land already named Bayham; we can be certain of this as 'the *hamm* or hemmed-in land of a man called Baega' has no mention of a place of worship. Eridge comes from *earn hrycg* and tells us this was once 'the ridge of land where eagles are seen'.

Three woods take their names from sources not seen as relating to woodland, hence all were transferred from existing names. Ruffet Wood took that of land known as 'the rough ground overgrown with furze'. Verridge Wood was associated with 'the bracken ridge'. With Stumlets Wood found near 'the place abounding in stumps', it shows there had been an earlier clearing of trees here.

Friston

The earliest known record of this name dates from 1200 and is exactly the same as today. This is 'the farmstead of a man called Freo', where the Saxon personal name is followed by *tun*.

One local name of interest is Hobb's Haste. Undoubtedly there was a family called Hobb here at one time but this does not explain the element 'Haste' until we find a record of Hobb's Arse in the 16th century. The meaning of 'arse' here is uncertain, although we can be sure it is not vulgar. Examples of the term are found elsewhere: one refers to where the eroded material from an extensive underground cave system is carried away to be deposited outside; another where streams act as natural sewers. Thus we should see the term to describe a place where unwanted material is removed. It is not clear exactly when 'Haste' replaced 'Arse', for although the last known use for the latter dates from the 16th century, it is several centuries before the present form appears. However, we can be certain the change was no accident, such 'cleaning up' of place names was commonplace, particularly in the Victorian era.

Glynde

Listed as Glinda in 1165, this name comes from Old English *glind* and describes the '(place of) the fenced enclosure'.

Here we find Farables Shaw, *fore* is an apple, one chosen for it ripens early.

Glyndebourne

A name which is linked to the previous entry and refers to 'the stream near Glynde'. Here Old English *burna* is added to the name defined previously and appears as Burne juxta Glynde in 1288.

Guestling

Listed as Gestelinges in the *Domesday* record of 1086, this is a Saxon personal name and Old English *inga* and describes the '(place of) the family or followers of a man called Gyrstel'.

Broomham comes from Old English *brom hamm* and tells us this was 'the hemmed-in land where broom grows'. Snailham shares the same suffix, here following *snaegl* and giving 'the hemmed-in land where snails abound'. Lidham

Guestling village sign.

Hill takes its name from a former settlement, here the Saxon personal name precedes the somewhat different *ham* to remind us of 'the homestead of a man called Hlyda'.

Guldeford, East

Listed as Est Gildeford in 1517, this name took the name of the lords of the manor who, in turn, took their name from Guildford in Surrey. The addition is to distinguish it from the family's town of origin.

H

Hadlow Down

A name not found before 1254 where it is documented as Hadleg. This form is a little late for us to be certain, however, this appears to come from Old English *haeth leah* and 'the woodland clearing where heather grows'.

What began as 'watery' names are now represented by two farms. Howbourne Farm took its name from 'the winding stream', while Loudwell Farm is still easily seen as 'the noisy spring'.

Hailsham

Listed as Hamelsham in 1086 and as Helesham in 1189, here a Saxon personal name and Old English *ham* refers to 'the homestead of a man called Haegel'.

Local names include Amberstone, the reference is not to the semi-precious amber but to the similarity in colour of 'the boundary stone'. Ersham Lodge is a fairly recent building on the estate which had long before had the name of 'the *hamm* or hemmed-in land of a man called Gifric'. Magham Down comes from *maecga ham* 'the homestead of the warrior or son'. Marland Bridge describes a scene from Saxon times, for this is 'the farmed land manured with marl'. Otham

Hadlow Down village sign.

Court takes a Saxon personal name with Old English *ham* as a lasting reminder of 'the homestead of a man called Otta'. Salt Marsh began describing 'the shallow marsh'.

Church of St Mark's at Hadlow Down.

The railway arrived in 1849, the so-called Cuckoo Line existing until the last train left at 22:30 on 8 September 1968. While the railway has gone it is not forgotten, for we still find the track as a cycle/footpath known as the Cuckoo Trail, Station Road has never been renamed, and both the Terminus and Railway Tavern public houses still welcome travellers, although never by rail.

Other public houses in the town begin with the Kings Head, here the sign depicts William the Conqueror but here is simply to show this was a loyal and patriotic establishment. The White Horse represents the House of Hanover, providing seven different monarchs. The White Hart is another which began as a 'royal' name, appearing when Richard II came to the throne in 1377. However, its continued popularity is down to its use as the generic name for all pubs.

The Corn Exchange is a reminder of how inns across the country connected a trade network which existed until the coming of the canals and later the railways. Licenced premises also acted as agents and temporary warehousing and it was commonplace, until the 19th century, for grains to be traded by both farmers and merchants. Other traders and craftsmen have given names to both the Bricklayers Arms and the Potters Arms. The Merrie Harriers would have started as a reference to the bird, a Marsh Harrier, any additional suggestion of jollity or happiness is an advertising tool.

Known locally as 'the Grenny', the Grenadier is named after the Grenadier Guards. Note how the original name referred to any soldier who was employed to throw grenades, although later it rather oddly was applied to the tallest and finest men of any regiment. The Golden Cross is a place name.

Most often the Lamb Inn points to an association with the church, the 'lamb' being Christ who is described as 'the Lamb of God' in John 1:29. The Yew Tree Inn would have been chosen to take advantage of this long-lived tree as a marker. Indeed the tree was associated with churches as they were planted to symbolise immortality.

Hamsey

Found as Hamme in 961, as Hame in 1086, and as Hammes Say in 1306. The basic name is from Old English *hamm* and refers to the 'hemmed in land', here the boundary is formed by a bend in the river. The addition is manorial, normally separate as in the 14th-century form, and refers to the de Say family who were here by the 13th century.

Minor names of this parish include Cooksbridge, this being home to the family of Thomas Coke by 1543. Hewenstreet Farm is from the Old English *hiwan straet*, literally 'the Roman road of the members of the community' and understood as 'the settlement at the good road'. Offham refers to 'the crooked hemmed-in land', the suffix *hamm* used to describe a place difficult to approach other than from one direction.

Hangleton

Listed as Hangetone in 1086, as Hangeltuna in 1115, and as Hengelton in 1248, the first element proves something of a problem. As none of the forms available contain the 'r' then *hangra* 'overhanging, a slope' can be discounted. However, the topography fits and thus is certainly related, although with the real word uncertain perhaps best defined as *hangelle tun* 'the farmstead at the hanging feature'.

Locally we find the Hangleton Manor, licenced premises occupying the old manor house. The minor name of Benfield Farm comes from Old English *beonet feld* or 'the open land where bent grass grows'.

Hankham

Listed as Hanecam hamme in 947 and as Henecham in 1086, this is 'the hemmed in land of a man called Haneca'. This is derived from Old English *hamm* and a Saxon personal name.

Hartfield

This place is recorded as Hertevel in *Domesday* and as Hertefeld in the 12th century. Here the name speaks of 'the open land frequented by harts of stags' and is derived from Old English *heorot feld*.

Chuck Hatch is a minor name which may produce an image of the place when defining it. The *haecc* or 'forest gate' here may have been where chucks were cut, the wedge or weight used much the same as a chuck, served as a brake under the wheels of an aeroplane on the ground. However, it is tempting to give this as the alternative, the chuck being a weight used to close the gate using gravity alone. Commonplace today, if this is the true origin then this could be the earliest example known.

Cotchford Farm refers to itself as 'the ford by a thicket'. Hodore Farm could be found near 'the heathy bank'. Puckstye Farm derives its name from *puca stig* meaning 'the steep path associated with a goblin'. Quabrook describes 'the boggy place at the brook'. While Tugmore Shaw speaks of 'the *ora* or bank associated with a man called Tucca'.

The pubs of Hartfield begin with the Hope and Anchor. Forget the sea, this is associated with Christianity and speaks of the hope that one's faith will prove an anchor through life. The Haywaggon Inn speaks for itself but note the spelling of 'waggon', still the preferred version according to the dictionary.

The Gallipot Inn and Gallipot Street share a common origin. One of the three cottages which eventually became the inn was home to those who produced small, glazed earthenware pots for storing medicines and salves. However, this was before the pub opened for business for the first time in 1597 during the reign of Elizabeth I. From the coat of arms of the Sackville family comes the Dorset Arms, these held the title earls of Dorset, their seat at nearby Buckhurst Park.

Hammerwood is a local name referring to the iron industry of the Weald. There are a number of ponds here, created to provide power to the watermills which then powered hammers, or bellows for forges and furnaces. At nearby Coleman Hatch is Poohsticks Bridge, named after the character in the books by A.A. Milne for this was where the author created the game with his son Christopher. Indeed it was Christopher Robin Milne who opened the newly named bridge when it was rebuilt in the 1970s. For those who have never heard of this pastime it involves two or more players, each then choosing their stick and standing on the upstream side of the bridge. At a given signal they drop (not throw) their stick into the water and then run to the opposite side of the bridge where they wait to see whose stick appears first and is thus the victor. Note when the game was played by father and son the original bridge was called Posingford Bridge.

Hastings

Recorded as Hastinges in the *Domesday* survey of 1086, this comes from a Saxon personal name and Old English *inga* telling of the '(place of) the family or followers of a man called Haesta'. However, this was not the original name of the place, for at the beginning of the 10th century we find Haestingaceaster or 'the Roman stronghold of Haesta's people'.

Street names in Hastings tell the history of this town, although we do find names seen in most places such as High Street, referring to its importance not its elevation, which was earlier known as Market Street, itself requiring no explanation. Similarly All Saints Street clearly took the dedication of the church here.

Early residents are seen in some places. Bachelor's Bump can be traced back to the 13th century when James Bachelarius was in residence. We know Barley Lane was named after John Barley, a mercer by trade, he was living here in 1601. Farmer John Benrigg is remembered by Bembrook Road, the spelling having changed over the intervening centuries.

With all the history associated with the place, Hastings' claim as the birthplace of television seems unusual.

Benefactors are often honoured by a street. Colonel Pelham, Member of Parliament for Hastings in the 18th century, gave his name to Pelham Square. Landowner Lord Cornwallis is commemorated by Cornwallis Gardens. Breeds Place stands on land developed by James Lansdell around 1828 and named after the woman he married, Martha Breeds. Carlisle Parade recalls Lord Carlisle, who was on the board of the group who owned the land.

Queen Caroline, consort of George IV, was the inspiration for Caroline Place while her daughter, Princess Charlotte, gave a name to Coburg Place after marrying Prince Leopold of Saxe-Coburg. Queen's Road honours Queen Victoria. De Cham Road is on land given to St Mary Magdalen Hosptial by Petronilla de Cham in 1294. Landowner Sir Howard Elphinstone is remembered by the name of Elphinstone Road. Pelham Crescent recalls Sir Thomas Pelham, 1st Earl of Chichester.

Local government officers are responsible for naming these streets in more recent times and thus it is no surprise to find their names on the signs at each end of these ways. Yet Theaklen Drive could never be considered undeserved, being a composite of the names of two councillors who brought a great deal of light industry to the town, D.B. Theaker and A.W. Lennard.

Collier Road remembers John Collier (1685–1760), known for his time as town clerk and serving five terms as mayor. Edward Milward Snr and Edward Milward Jnr both served as local officials in the 18th century, one or perhaps both are the reason for the naming of Milward Road. Robertson Street recalls former member of parliament P.F. Robertson, elected in 1857.

Ebenezer Road took the name of the Ebenezer Baptist Chapel here. The Reverend William Parker, rector of All Saints and founder of Hastings Grammar School's work for the town is commemorated in Parker Road. Old Roar Road takes its name from the waterfall known as Old Roar Ghyll. Old Humphrey Avenue was named after George Mogridge who died at his home here and was known as Old Humphrey.

Mercers Bank recalls one of the towns most important trades. Former linen draper James Halloway's establishment was in Halloway Place. Salter's Lane is the site of an old salthouse, once the most important of commodities. Tripe Alley was where the butchers were in the habit of throwing the offal after butchering the carcasses. It is today known as Sinnock's Square, this prominent local family first seen in the St Clements church records of 1598 when Emannual Sennock married.

There are always some which have a unique origin and few can be more different than Bohemia Road. Nothing unusual about the source, it was taken from Bohemia House which stood here before any other building on this road. It is the origin of how the house acquired the name which makes this so unusual. It may be seen as quintiscentially English to name one's home from the practice of taking tea outside, it being referred to as 'bohemia fashion'. Tackleway is nothing to do with fishing, this place is recorded as Le Tegillwey in 1499, this showing it was named because it was literally 'tiled' understood as 'paved'.

Crown Lane was named after the Crown Inn here, similarly George Lane gave a name to the George Inn, and the Swan pub is remembered by Swan Place. The Bo-Peep public house was erroneously given as 'Bossup' on a map in the 18th century, although a document dated 1746 gave it as Bo-Peep House. This name is derived directly from what is now considered a young child's game of peep-o, named as it was the known haunt of smugglers.

Baldslow is a local name derived from a Saxon personal name with Old English *hlaw*. Together these give us 'the hill of a man called Beald'. Bulverhythe has two Old English elements, from *burhwara hythe* this is 'the landing place of the citizens'. Gensing derives its name from its inhabitants, the '(place) of the people of a man called Genesa'.

Public houses of this coastal town begin with the Royal Albion, borrowing a name from the Royal Albion Hotel and thus the name we need to define. Originally the Albion Hotel, it took its name from the Latin name for Britain, a reference to the white cliffs of the south coast here. When extended in 1847 it acquired the addition, although we have no record of a royal guest.

The Prince Albert was named after the consort of Queen Victoria, she was not only a queen but an empress, the adjective describing such seen in the name of the Imperial. Another royal gave his name to the Old King John, the infamous King John, who earned himself the soubriquet Lackland, set his seal to the *Magna Carta*.

The Clarence Hotel recalls the Duke of Clarence, the man who was to become William IV on the death of his brother, George IV. William IV is the image seen on the sign outside the Kings Head, while his wife and consort, born of the house of Saxe-Meiningen, is remembered by the Queen Adelaide. For those who can read heraldic imagery the royal standard displays a sign which tells a great family history without using a single letter or punctuation mark. Outside the Royal Standard at Hastings we see that used by the Duke of Normandy, later William I of England.

A Royal Charter of 1155 established five ports which should maintain ships so as to be ready to react to any threat from the sea at any time. Issued by the Normans it named five ports, the French for 'five' being *cinq* hence the name of the Cinque Ports public house. However, this should never be pronounced in the French manner but has been Anglicised to 'sink'. The five were Hastings, Romney, Dover, Hythe, and Sandwich, although today only Hastings and Dover are still working ports, the remainder having silted up. Today a ceremonial office, the title of Lord Warden of the Cinque Ports is normally held by a member of the royal family or prime minister, particularly those associated with our nation in times of war. The Lord Warden pub shares this title.

In this coastal location the Dolphin Inn has to be a maritime reference. To sailors the dolphin was their friend, even said to have wound their bodies around an anchor chain to prevent drag during a storm. Undoubtedly the most famous maritime hero our nation has ever produced, the Lord Nelson is just one of the pubs which honour the man who has more pubs named after him than any other individual.

Said to be the second oldest pub in Hastings, the Anchor has a very different origin from the usual, a symbol representing the Christian faith. Today the pub is some distance from the sea and yet once the water came much further inland. Indeed the local belief is this name derives from the boats which could moor almost at the front door.

The Havelock in Havelock Road share an origin in Sir Henry Havelock, an English soldier who was a hero of the Indian Mutiny and who led the British forces at the relief of Lucknow but then sadly died two months later. The Heroes pub is in the same street. Another famous military man is remembered by the Duke of Wellington.

Known as the Swedish nightingale, the Jenny Lind remembers the 19th-century songstress who earned fame on tours of Europe and America. John Logie Baird died at nearby Bexhill. Once a household name, in the digital age it is often forgotten that this Scotsman developed the first practical working television system. At sea at the beginning of the 19th century, the *London Tavern* gave its name to the pub which depicts this vessel in full sail.

The Stag certainly began as an heraldic device, a popular image used by many powerful families. While the Crown is easier to see as an indication this was a royal supporter and a patriot. There is little doubt in the origins of Ye Olde Pump House, a grade two listed building and one of the few remaining buildings of the old town. Sometimes referred to by the acronym FILO, a name adopted by the micro-brewery working out of here, the First In Last Out refers to its location in the old town, the first pub encountered on the way in to Hastings has to be the last chance for a pint on the way out.

Picture a man carrying two small barrels tied together with a length of rope in a form of a harness and slung over the shoulders. This is the image of a smuggler, he who carried the contraband from the shore inland and who gave his name to the Tubman. The Smugglers is a more obvious reference, while the

Cutter is a single-masted vessel favoured by the excise men when after smugglers at sea.

The Pigs in Paradise suggests this may be a highly sought after establishment, although the more common phrase would not use 'paradise'! The Dripping Well is named after a nearby spring. Both the Priory and the Whitefriars, and also Priory Road, are all clear links to this being church land, an origin shared by the Angel Inn. Premises named the Oddfellows Arms show this to be a meeting place for the Independent Order of Oddfellows, a friendly society founded in the 19th century with branches in several countries.

The Malvern is on Malvern Way, one of several roads here named after a range of hills and including Cotswold Close, The Cheviots, Mendip Gardens, Chiltern Drive, and Pennine Rise. The Clown pays tribute to a famous clown of this time, Joseph Grimaldi (1779–1837). A family who have produced generations of statesmen and politicians are the earls Granville, a name adopted by the Granville Tavern. Former prime minister Benjamin Disraeli, Earl of Beaconsfield, is commemorated in the name of the Beaconsfield. Note this should be pronounced 'beckon-' not 'beacon-'. The Shah is a reminder of the state visit of the Shah of Persia to Britain in 1887.

Carlisle is about as far away from Hastings as it is possible to be, hence the pub of this name clearly has a different origin. Here the Carlisle is a reminder of the Howard family, dukes of Norfolk who were also earls of Carlisle. The Fountain Hotel is derived from an heraldic device seen in the crest of the Master Mariners. Brother of William the Conqueror and a man who built Hastings Castle, is recalled by the Robert de Mortaine.

Heathfield

A name derived from Old English *haeth feld* and 'the open land where heather grows'. The name is recorded as Hadfeld in the 12th century.

Beckington Farm comes from a Saxon personal name followed by *ing tun*, this describing 'the farmstead associated with a man called Becca'. This pattern is repeated for Runtington Farm and Sapperton Farm, giving 'the farmstead asssociated with a man called Hrunta' and 'the farmstead associated with a man called Saebeorht' respectively. Tottingworth has the suffix *worth* and speaks of 'the enclosure of a man called Totta'. While in the case of Pigstrood it is *strod* warning of 'the marshy land covered by brushwood of a man called Bica'.

Markly is from *meare leah*, Old English for 'the woodland clearing at or near the marshland'. Cade Street is a corruption, possibly through a family name, of 'cart' and is self-explanatory. Bingletts Wood takes the name of the clearings, where the dialect term *bing* precedes *leahs* to tell us of 'the woodland clearings marked by heaps'.

Pub names begin with the Gun Inn, located on Gun Hill and was once the main court house for the area. The Horam Inn takes a minor place name. Location is also the reason for the May Garland Inn, May Day celebrations have been passed down from pre-Christian times. The Star Inn is a 14th-century building with a name derived from its location adjacent to the village church, this being an image associated with the Star of Bethlehem and symbolising the Virgin Mary.

Cross-in-Hand is a hamlet named from the pub, the name held to be a reminder of the year 1547 when men met here before embarking on a Crusade to the Holy Land. The Half Moon today shows a crescent moon, however, it seems reasonable to believe this was originally lying on its back and thus related to the previous name. Such an image was adopted as a device in the arms of families whose ancestors were known to have fought in the Crusades.

Royal names include the Prince of Wales, a general reference to the title rather than to one holder of same. Similarly the Crown shows support for the

Cross In Hand Inn's sign shows this to be a reference to St George, patron saint of England.

The Horam Inn, Heathfield.

monarchy. The Swan is also probably taken from a coat of arms, the majestic bird having been adopted by many, including Henry VIII and Edward III. The product is seen in the name of the Brewers Arms and also the Barley Mow, this being a stack of one of the most important ingredients in brewing.

The Three Cups is an heraldic image used by the Worshipful Company of Salters. However, here traditionally this name is held to be local dialect referring to the source of a stream, there being a trio of such here. The Horse and Groom is an advertisement for services offered to both the rider and his mount.

Outside the Runt-in-tun is the image of a small pig seated in a large barrel, a seemingly perfect representation of the name. However, the real origin can be seen just up the road for this represents an approximation of the pronunciation of Runtington Farm, a name defined above.

The Jack Cade is named after the leader of the revolt in 1450. Increasingly unpopular, Henry VI fled when Cade led a band of some 5,000 in a march on London. On reaching the capital the mob resorted to looting but were eventually defeated at London Bridge and they fled. Officially all were offered a pardon and promised action on their demands for reforms, effectively this was simply a ruse to get them to reveal themselves and most were declared traitors. Their charismatic leader, Cade, was trapped and killed in a minor skirmish near Lewes on 12 July that year.

Heighton, South

Recorded as Hectone in 1086 and as Sutheghton in 1327, this name comes from Old English *heah tun*, with the later addition of *suth*, together describing 'the southern high farmstead'.

There is no record of a North Heighton, which raises the question of why this place is not simply Heighton. There are two possible explanations, the most obvious being Heighton Hill which is indeed to the north of here. However, so is

Norton and with the hill clearly being named from this village it seems probably that both have influenced the adddition here.

During World War Two a series of tunnels connected Denton House in South Heighton with HMS *Forward*, a shore establishment of the Royal Navy. This secret establishment complimented the coastal radar chain in monitoring all traffic in the English Channel between Dungeness and Selsey. The maze of tunnels still exists some 66 feet beneath most of the village. Today Denton House has been converted into flats and a road built capable of allowing traffic. That road was named Forward Road to commemorate the efforts of those working here during the war.

The Hampden Arms is derived from land held by Robert Hampden Trevor, 1st Viscount Hampden (1706–83). The family were based in Buckinghamshire: Robert a politician, diplomat and amateur architect; his brother Richard became Bishop of Durham.

Hellingly

Listed as Hellingeleghe in the 13th century, there are two possible origins of this Old English name. If this is *hyll inga leah* it speaks of 'the woodland clearing of the hill dwellers', or if the first element is a Saxon personal name then 'the woodland clearing of the family or followers of a man called Hielle'.

Boship Farm is from the Old English term *geburscipe* which, as stated in the Laws of Edward the Elder, is specifically an association or community of peasants'. Thus this could be said to be an early example of a workers' co-operative. Horselunges has two parts, the first *hyrst* is from 'a wooded hill', the latter a reminder of the family of William de Lyngyver who were here in 1318.

Dicker comes from the Middle English *dyker*, the word existing today as the prefix 'deca' and having the same meaning 'ten'. The question remains, 10 what? It is certainly not a land measurement, the area is far too small. However, it was where ore was once smelted, so perhaps this is a reference to the number of furnaces or even the number of rods of iron in the bundle, packed ready for despatch.

Herstmonceux

Listed as Herst in 1086, the simplest form of the name comes from Old English *hyrst* 'wooded hill'. Later, in 1287, we see Herstmnceus, the addition being a reminder of the Monceux family who were here by the 12th century.

Three minor names of note here, the first two have probably influenced one another in terms of pronunciation and thus spelling, although in reality they are quite different. Chilsham is derived from the suffix *ham* and a Saxon personal name to speak of 'the homestead of a man called Ceolwig'. Chilthurst combines *cild* in a plural form and *hyrst* and describes 'the wooded hill of the young noblemen'.

Cowbeech refers to 'pollarded beech trees' and reveals a little more of daily life in this area. Pollarding is similar to coppicing in that the tree is cut right back, all branches and leaves removed. This encourages fresh growth in the form of straight and strong poles, used in the construction of the framework of most buildings and fences. The only difference between coppicing and pollarding is the height, the former is cut to a mere stump, in the latter case the trunk is cut above the highest reach of browsers which would otherwise feast on the tender new shoots. This tells us the woodland was not only managed but their animals were allowed to graze and forage on the ground. Hence by defining a place name we have an instant image of life in the Saxon era.

Public houses of Herstmonceux begin with the Bulls Head, almost certainly taken from an heraldic image. However this powerful image is found in many coats of arms, from the smallest landholder to the pope, hence is difficult to find the true origin. Conversely in the case of the Brewers Arms the name is quite obvious.

The Woolpack is also symbolic, a reminder of the days when England's wealth was based on its wool trade. Prior to the canals and the railways, pack horses on bad roads were the sole method of transport inland. A woolpack was the large bale of wool weighing 240 pounds, a common sight at inns on the large distribution network. Those thirsty men who transported the bales would have looked forward to a stop at an inn, while those who were simply passing by were invited inside by the name of the Welcome Stranger.

Hoathly, East

A name found as simply Hodlegh in 1287, the name comes from Old English *hath leah* and describes 'the woodland clearing where heather grows'.

Scallow is from *calu*, Old English for 'smooth, bare'. This should not be taken literally, the description of the ground here is probably only a reference to poor soil and sparse growth. Whyly is very different in being a most desirable place, not for agricultural purposes but as 'the clearing where heathen rites are practised'.

Two pubs here; the Foresters Arms announces itself as a meeting place, known as a 'lodge' or 'court', for the Ancient Order of Foresters. This large friendly society have branches across not only the United Kingdom but also the United States of America. While the Kings Head is often simply a show of support for the monarchy, here the sign depicts the unmistakeable image of Charles I. This could never have been here during the Interregnum, the period when the nation had no monarch from 1649-60 and this name would certainly not have been allowed under the Protectorate of Oliver Cromwell. Hence this sign shows support for the monarchy at or following the Restoration.

Hollington

Domesday lists this name as Holintune in 1086. Derived from Old English *holegn tun* this is 'the farmstead where holly grows'.

Some of Hooe's history captured in a single image.

Harley Road passes 'the woodland clearing frequented by hares' from Old English *hara leah*. Wilting Farms gets its name from the '(place) of the people of Wilta'.

Hooe

Domesday lists this name as Hou, while the original Old English is *hoh* describing the '(place at) the spur of land'.

Horsted, Little

Seen as Horstede in *Domesday*, as with the previous entry this is *hors stede* 'the place where horses are kept'. The addition, to distinguish from the previous entry, appears as Little Horstede in 1307, the same document in which the addition is first seen for the previous entry also.

One minor name here, that of Hunnington's Farm. Old English *inga tun* follows a Saxon personal name and tells us this was once 'the farmstead of the family or followers of a man called Huna'.

Hove

First seen as La Houue in 1288, here is Old English *hufe* referring to 'the hood shaped hill'. The same word is also seen to describe a 'shelter', so perhaps this is how the name should be understood.

Goldstone Barn is a modern name, it refers to a mass of breccia deliberately buried in the 19th century. Goldstone is best known as the former home ground of the local professional football team.

Pub names begin with the Bell, showing this is associated with the church and with St Andrews Primary School opposite on land owned by the church. As the third son of Queen Victoria, Prince Arthur was granted the title Duke of Connaught and Strathearn. His title remembered by the Connaught public house.

The Downsman clearly intends to offer hospitality to those living on and around the South Downs. However, there is no official description of a 'downsman' and it looks to have been created to correspond with the northern 'dalesman'.

The Stirling Arms is probably a reference to the Alexander family, earls of Stirling, although this line has been extinct since the death of the fifth earl in 1739. On Rutland Road is found the Rutland Arms, presumably the road came first and both taking the name of the dukes of Rutland. The dukes of Portland gave their name to the Portland Hotel. On Nevill Road is the Nevill public house, both sharing an origin in the name of the family who became earls of Lewes.

Brunswick is a nearby district name and is referred to in two pub names as the Brunswick and also the Wick Inn. Similarly a place name is also seen in the Hove Inn and also the Sussex, while the Albion, the Latin name for Britain, is derived

Statue marking the work of Edward VII in the development of Hove.

from the white cliffs for which Sussex is famous. Aldrington is a minor name referring to 'the farmstead of the family or followers of a man called Ealdhere' and seen today in the Aldrington public house.

Location would have been the inspiration for the Neptune, the Roman god of the sea, while the Ancient Mariner links to the ocean while taking the name of the famous poem *The Rime of the Ancient Mariner* by Samuel Taylor Coleridge. Offering a welcome to travellers, the Station could not have been named until the coming of the railways.

A local entertainer known as Blind Harry was a popular entertainer on these streets in the late 19th century; he is remembered by the Blind Busker. Hove is home to the county cricket team, hence the name of the Sussex Cricketer. Still the most common pub name in England, the Red Lion symbolises a connection to Scotland.

The Eclipse has three different origins. Some refer to a famous stagecoach, others to the astronomical spectacle when the sun is darkened for a few brief moments by the passing of the moon between it and the earth. However, here the name is taken from the Eclipse Stakes, a flat race for horses aged three years and above which is run every July at Sandown Park over a distance of one mile, two furlongs and seven yards.

The Slug and Lettuce, today the name of a chain of pub/restaurants, is said to have begun as a pub name many years ago when a miserly landlord was looking for the best deal for his new pub sign. A local offered to paint the sign in return for free ale, but when the sign was hanging outside others could not see what it represented. "It's a cow in a field!" cried the landlord. "Looks more like a slug and lettuce" replied a customer. A nice story but one which must be an example of creative etymology.

Beginning as a skilled worker in stone in medieval times, the Freemasons Tavern is a reminder of the trade where skills were closely guarded. Hence what we would today refer to as a 'closed shop' existed to prevent cowboy builders giving these highly skilled men a bad name. Today we associate the term with a fraternal society who, while still operating under a cover of secrecy, are known to give their time and efforts generously to charitable works and would indicate this was a meeting place for freemasons.

The Iron Duke was a nickname given to the Arthur Wellesley, Duke of Wellington who is most often associated with victory over Napoleon at Waterloo. This pairing is seen here also, with the pub named after the British commanding officer and the road in which it stands, Waterloo Street. Another military leader is suggested in the name of the Conqueror, although here the reference is to William, Duke of Normandy who became King of England in 1066.

Few will be unaware the Bow Street Runner was a name applied to the fledgling police force in this country. Yet few will realise it originally referred to just eight individuals who were empowered by Bow Street Court in London, the term later used to describe early law enforcement officers in general. However, these men, recognised by the red waistcoats that earned them the name 'robin redbreasts', were actually the origin of the CID.

Anyone named Cooper will be aware their surname derives from a craftsman skilled in the production of barrels, casks and tubs from wooden staves and metal hoops. Today such containers are invariably associated with wines and beers, hence the origin of the Cooper's Cask. A large cask of indeterminate volume for wines and beers advertises the product in both the sign and name of the Hogshead.

I

Icklesham

A name recorded as Icoleshamme in 770 and derived from a Saxon personal name and Old English *hamm* refers to 'the hemmed-in land of a man called Icel'.

Local names include Linthurst, from Old English *lind hyrst* or 'the wooded hill of lime trees'. The Roughter has changed little since it began as 'the rough enclosure'.

Pubs here include the Queens Head which has a excellent recorded history. The buildings, for this was originally two adjoining cottages, were built in 1632 during the reign of Charles I. It did sell beers until 1831 when swine keeper William Goodwin bought himself a beer license for the princely sum of two guineas. After another two owners came and went, the Star Brewery of Eastbourne acquired the place in 1853 and named it the Queens Head after Queen Victoria.

The Robin Hood is a popular pub name for it is reminiscent of the popular hero of folklore. However, as a pub name it is comparatively recent, given to the image of a woodsman who wore clothing similar to that of the legendary Merrie Men of Sherwood Forest.

Iden

Domesday's record of Idene is little different to the modern form but somewhat different to the original Old English *ig denn* and telling of 'the woodland pasture where yew trees grow'.

The local name of Bosney describes 'the enclosure of a man called Bosa', the Saxon name followed by Old English *gehaeg.*

The Bell at Iden leaves no doubt where the pub is found, nor that it has associations with the church.

Iford

A name recorded as Niworde in *Domesday* and as Yford in the late 11th century. Here are two possible meanings where Old English *ieg ford* or *ig ford* give 'the ford in well-watered land' or 'the ford where yew trees grow' respectively.

Minor place names include Swanborough Farm, this tells us it got its name from a reference to 'the hill of the peasants'. Harvey's Cross is of much more recent derivation, it marks a spot where a man named Harvey fell and died while hunting in 1821.

Isfield

Listed as Isefeld in 1214, this is from Old English *feld* and a Saxon personal name and describing 'the open land of a man called Isa'. Local legend maintains King Harold spent the night of 13 October 1066 here, the eve of the Battle of Hastings.

Hookgrove Wood may have changed over the centuries since Saxon times, yet the name has changed little. Indeed it is still possible to recognise this as 'the woodland grove on the hook of land'.

The Halfway House is an old coaching inn, its name showing it was a resting point for humans and horses alike on the road between Maresfield and Lewes. A second pub in the village requires further investigation, for it has had three names. It began as the Half Moon, the landlord brought the name with him from his previous establishment, before offering a welcome to travellers as the Station Hotel when the railway arrived in the 1850s. In 1957 incoming landlord Arnold Russell wished to change the name and, apparently inspired by this being the headquarters of the Isfield and District Angling Club, changed the name of the pub to the Laughing Fish. Shortly afterwards the new landlord installed the plate glass seen in the front of the pub, acquired from a recently closed fish and chip shop in Eastbourne. While Mr Russell's idea for 'fish' likely suggested itself by the angling club, he also being a keen fisherman, it seems convenient the pane of glass with a very happy fish appeared soon after his arrival, so perhaps the smiling fish was suggested by the image on the glass.

Jevington

Found in *Domesday* as Lovingetone and as Govingetone in 1189, here is a Saxon personal name and Old English *inga tun* giving 'the farmstead of the family or followers of a man called Geofa'.

Filching Manor occupies land already named well before this place was constructed. Here is a Saxon place name which suggests it has long been the focus of the settlements. The earliest forms show an uncertain personal name with Old English *inga* giving the '(place) associated with a man called Fylca or Folca'. A similiar construction is seen in Teddard's Barn, a corruption of 'the *worth* or enclosure of a man called Teoda'. Wannock has few early forms but may be derived from an old stream name, in which case this would be referring to 'the little wan one'. The Eight Bells public house is named for it being associated with the church, this being the usual number of bells in a peal.

The annual Jevington Fete is held at Filching Manor, where the Campbell Circuit is a karting track named after the late Donald Campbell who broke speed records on both land and sea. All his racers were called *Bluebird*, the second speedboat *Bluebird II*, is the sole remaining example and is on display at the local museum and the subject of a long-term restoration project.

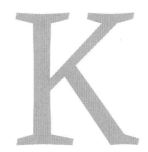

Kent (Ditch and Water)

Two water courses linked by a common line, the traditional boundary between Sussex and Kent. Kent Ditch was formerly known as Mylryve from Old English *mill rive* the latter meaning literally 'rife' and understood as 'plentiful', hence a very profitable mill. Kent Water was previously known as Le Blok, a name meaning 'the pale of shining one'.

Kingston near Lewes

Found as Kinredeford in 1228, the basic name comes from a Saxon personal name and Old English *ford* tell of 'the ford of a woman called Cynethryth or of a man called Cynered'. The additional Lewes, to distinguish this from the previous entry, is discussed under its own entry.

Nan Kemp's Cottage is said to have been home to a particularly unsavoury woman. She is said to have welcomed home her hungry husband from the fields with a filling pie. However, it later transpired the meaty pie contained a filling made from their murdered child. Mrs Kemp was hanged and buried somewhere at the top end of Ashcombe Lane; her spirit was said to appear if you circled her grave three times with your eyes tightly shut.

Kingston seems to attract dubious characters for another character spoken of was one Martin Brown. Having deserted from the Royal Horse Artillery he turned to petty crime to supplement his meagre earnings as a farm labourer. On the farm his loathing for a shepherd named Tuppen was common knowledge, although why his disliked him so much was never recorded. Brown lay in wait for Tuppen one dark night, shooting dead the man as he passed. However, the dead man was not Tuppen but David Baldey, his employer. Brown was hanged in December 1868 at the prison in Lewes aged just 22.

A unique pub name is found here in the Juggs Arms. Not a misspelling of the pint pot with a handle, this is held to be a dialect term for the men who brought fish from Brighton to Lewes using carrying baskets.

Langney

Listed as Langelie in 1086 and as Langania in 1121, this is from Old English *lang eg* and describes 'the long piece of dry ground in a marsh'.

Laughton

A fairly common name which is derived from Old English *leac tun* telling of 'the farmstead of the leeks or vegetables'. The name is recorded as Lestone in *Domesday* and is understood to be referring to a market garden.

Vert Wood has nothing to do with the French word for 'green', indeed quite the reverse in its meaning of 'scrubland' or 'sparse vegetation'. An even less inviting name is that or Terrible Down, which can be traced back to the origin of 'at the dung hill'.

The local is the Roebuck Inn, possibly a reference to one of the only two native species of deer, the roe deer. However, it is also used extensively in heraldry, almost always with the image of the male or buck, which does seem more likely here.

Lewes

Found as Laewus in 961 and as Lewes in 1086, this name represents Old English *hlaew* in a plural form and telling of 'the burial mounds'.

Street names of Lewes include Brooman's Lane and Ireland's Lane, which can be traced back to 1352 and 1624 respectively, when the families of Ralph Bronman and John Ireland were living here. Two very different references are found in Rotten Row and Spital Road, both are quite common and found in many towns around the country and always with the same meaning. It does not take much imagination to see Spital Road originating in the Hospital of St Nicholas, similarly Rotten Row is always a derogatory name.

Cockshut Road is an old place name, one common to many places around England and always with the same meaning. Our meat diet was previously much more varied, virtually anything was considered potential protein for the pot. Birds were not easy to catch in flight, thus a method was developed where a large net was stretched across one end of a woodland clearing. By approaching from the opposite side of the clearing the birds would naturally take flight and head for the trees away from the hunters only to become entangled in the net.

This method was particularly popular when catching woodcock, a ground nesting bird whose perfect camouflage and lack of scent made it impossible to detect by either the man or his dog unless put to flight. Considered a delicacy, this was not eaten but sold to the house of the lord of the manor.

Baxter Road was the location for the printing business founded by John Baxter. The Lee family moved their printing business into the town in 1938; this is marked by Lee Road. Foundry Lane was the site of an iron and brass foundry in the 19th century, owned by Ebenezer Morris. Mr Pope was an 18th-century chemist, his name found in Pope's Passage. Richard Evershed set up his business in 1810, both the location and nature of the business recalled by the later naming of Soap Factory Lane.

English's Passage was home to the prominent English family, certainly here by 1768. Fisher Street is probably after William Fysher who owned this land in 1340. Horsfield Road recalls Unitarian minister Thomas Walker Horsfield, here from 1817 to 1837. From the Spences House home of Quakeress Miss Rickman comes the name of Spences Lane.

John Stansfield was a prominent citizen from at least 1624, hence the naming of Stansfield Road. Walwers Lane is a reminder of the family resident in Lewes for several generations. Christie Road recalls John Christie, who is famous as the founder of Glyndebourne Festival Opera House. On a similar note Mildmay Road marks the talents of opera singer Audrey Mildmay.

Evelyn Road remembers John Evelyn, an author, diarist and friend of Samuel Pepys, he was treasurer of Greenwich Hospital. Serving as member of parliament for Lewes in the 19th century, Henry Fitzroy gave his name to Fitzroy Road. John Lancaster founded many schools and certainly merits the honour of Lancaster Street named after him.

Two local councillors are commemorated by the naming of roads. Crisp Road recalls the Alderman Charles Doland Crisp OBE, while Councillor D. J. Fitzgerald saw his name at both ends of Fitzgerald Road.

The Lynchets is from a Middle English term describing the terracing formed by repeatedly ploughing the same way along the land. Blois Road is a reminder the town is twinned with Blois in France. While the town is not twinned with the US state of Delaware, there is a place called Lewes in Delaware.

The prime meridian, the line of longitude which forms the basis for every clock in the world is also known as the Greenwich Meridian. Not surprisingly the borough of Greenwich was the first to recognise its existence and yet the line continues south to run through Eastbourne, there being no doubt which line it follows as the path is shown by the name Meridian Road. There is also a Meridian public house.

The Lewes Arms needs no explanation, the Pump House points to such being found nearby. Location is also relevant in the Swan, most likely a reference to the birds which will have been seen here on the River Ouse since the first settlement was founded.

Pubs also include those named after the nobility. The Kings Head featuring the unmistakeable image of King Henry VIII. The Royal Oak remembers the flight of Charles II when he hid in the Boscobel Oak to evade capture, while the Crown Inn is a general show of support for the monarchy, a patriotic sign.

Other individuals include the John Harvey Tavern. This is one of 50 or so houses belonging to the Harveys Brewery – the lack of a possessive apostrophe would seem to be deliberate it is not found on official paperwork at any time in over 200 years – which was founded by John Harvey as the Bridge Wharf Brewery in the 18th century.

Heraldry is always a favourite and explains why there are so many coloured animals in pub names including the Black Horse. Best known as the image used by a well-known bank, it is also the nickname of the 7th Dragoon Guards, the goldsmiths of London, and countless families. The Black Lion produces similar problems, the most common being Queen Philippa of Hainault, consort of Edward III although there is no known connection between her and this part of the country.

The sign featuring the emblem outside the Dorset Arms remembers the Sackville family, dukes of Dorset. The Pelham Arms is for the dukes of Newcastle, once major landholders. The arms of the Cutlers' Company features an elephant with a howdah, the origin of the Elephant and Castle. The Lamb is a reference to the church, Christ being referred to as 'the Lamb of God'. The first Gardeners Arms may well have been chosen originally by someone who worked the gardens of a larger estate.

Using the sign, and thus the name, to advertise the product was how the pub sign developed. When ales were brewed at home such was offered to travellers by tying a sheaf of barley to an ale stake, usually the trunk of a tree where all lower branches have been removed. Today another obvious name is found in the Brewers Arms.

The Volunteer most often can be traced back to the volunteer regiments of the 18th century to defend the nation under threat of invasion by the French under Napoleon. Tally Ho is a phrase associated with hunting, but here the name refers to a famous stagecoach which would have stopped here.

A subtle invitation is offered by the Rainbow, a reference to the story of the proverbial pot of gold being found at the end of the rainbow. Outside the Five Bells is an image of a ship's wheel, a pointer to this originating is the time signals used at sea. Sailors will know five bells as 2:30, 6:30, and 10:30 (both am and pm) although here we are only concerned with the first and the last which were once the closing times of the two sessions (excepting Sundays) before the relaxation of licencing laws. It could be argued the Six Bells refers to the opening time of 11am, however, it more likely points to the bells of the nearby church.

The Snowdrop refers to a specific date, 27 December 1836. That winter had been particularly harsh, and a build up of snow produced the worst recorded avalanche in Britain. Having built up on a nearby cliff the snow slipped on to cottages in what is now South Street. Of the 15 buried, eight people lost their lives.

The Chalk Pit Inn began life as the offices for the mining operation. Following extraction and removal along an ingenious funicular railway, the chalk was burnt in kilns and transported to the Ouse where a distribution system took the resulting lime across the county where it was used as a fertiliser.

Litlington

Found as Litlinton in a document from 1191, there are two possible origins for this Old English place name. If this represents *lytel tun* then this is 'the small farmstead' or, if the first element is a Saxon personal name, the name is 'the farmstead of a man called Lytela'.

The Plough and Harrow has two elements connected by 'and', the classic form for an English pub name. Here the rural location is reflected in the chosen name which, in its early days, would have attracted those who worked the land with images of the plough which exposed the subsoil and the harrow, which breaks up the clumps of earth into a fine tilth.

Lullington

Records of this name include Lullinton in 1192, Lollinton in 1193, and as Loynton in 1582. Here a Saxon personal name precedes Old English *inga tun*, this referring to 'the farmstead of the family or followers of a man called Lulla'.

Locally we find Plonk Barn, a name which described its construction as 'made from planks'.

M

Malling, South

The basic name here comes from Old English *inga* and a Saxon personal name telling of the '(place of) the family or followers of a man called Mealla'. This name is recorded as Mallingum in 818 and as Mellinges in 1086. The addition distinguishes it from a similar minor place name nearby.

Bridgwick Pit was dug out on land which already bore the name meaning 'the *wic* of a man called Beorht'. Old English *wic* should correctly be defined as 'specialised farm', although invariably that speciality is dairy produce. Chalkham Farm features the element *scealc ham*, Old English for 'the homestead of the servant'. Oxteddle Bottom is a lower area once 'frequented by oxen' and derived from *oxen seten*.

Bible Bottom, again a lower region, has a very odd history indeed. This feature is an earthwork, one which bears an uncanny resemblance to an open book and of course the best-selling book of all time is the good book. However, this was not the original name, it was deliberately changed from the original Devil's Book. Not that there was any satanic worship here, at least this was not the reason for the name. Earthworks were often associated with the Devil.

Maresfield

The earliest surviving record of this name dates from 1234 as Mersfeld. This is a little late for us to be certain of the Old English origin, thus we offer two alternatives. Either this is *mersc feld* 'the open land by the marsh' or *mere feld* and 'the open land by the pool'.

Maresfield's village sign tells something of its history.

Batt's Bridge took the name of nearby resident William Batte, yet the bridge was here before him when, not surprisingly, it was known by a different name. Breedenbridge being a more descriptive name, the first element represents *bredes* or 'planks'. The first part of Chelwood Vetchery speaks of 'the wood of a man named Ceola', the latter a common French addition describing 'a dairy farm'. The suffix of Prickett's Hatch is *haecc* meaning 'hatch gate', while early forms seem to point to *pricket* 'a young deer' the more likely first element is *pricker* or 'forester'.

At the Chequers Inn is a sign with origins as far back as the Roman era, with evidence found by archaeologists in the remains of Pompeii. Originally it showed a game similar to draughts was played within but later the same sign was used to indicate a moneyer. Today the word 'exchequer' is still associated with finances, the Chancellor of the Exchequer taking care of the nation's accounts from 11 Downing Street.

Mayfield

Listed as Magawelda in the 12th century, this Old English place name comes from *maegthe feld* and describes 'the open land where mayweed grows'.

Bivelham began as 'the *hamm* or hemmed-in land of a man called Bifela'. Isenhurst literally describes 'the iron wooded hill' but should be understood as where iron was smelted. Although the fire was not from burning the wood, this would simply not produce a high enough temperature. The relevant reference is the hill, one which would produce a natural updraught and mean less pumping of bellows to smelt the ore.

Bainden is the modern version of what began as 'the *denu* or swine pasture of a man called Baega'. Miss Cottages took the name of one Nicholas le Mist, whose family were here before 1327. Pennybridge Farm shows it is on land where there was an old toll bridge. Sharden Farm describes 'the dung swine pasture', from

St Bartholomew's Church, Maresfield.

scitten den. Spitlye originates from Old English *sped leah*, this speaking of 'the woodland clearing bringing great prosperity'. Unfortunately what brought that fortune is unrecorded.

Pubs here begin with the Middle House, a grade I listed Elizabethan building which was once home to Sir Thomas Gresham, keeper of the Privy Purse. Its name describes the location in the centre of the high street. Five Ashes is a minor place name derived from a number of ash trees. Trade names are always popular, although whether the pub named the Carpenters Arms is an invitation to those in one of the oldest trades or represents a former career of a landlord or owner will never be clear. However, there is no doubt as to the origins of the Rose and Crown, the latter shows support for the monarchy and the former means this is a patriot.

Medway, River

Listed as Medeuuage in the eighth century. The name is derived from a Celtic term *medu wey* telling of 'the river with sweet water'.

Moulsecoomb

Recorded at the end of the 11th century as Mulescumba, this features a Saxon personal name and Old English *cumb* and tells of 'the valley of a man called Mul'.

Mountfield

Seen as Montifelle in *Domesday* and as Mundifeld in the 12th century. Here the Saxon personal name is suffixed by Old English *feld* and speaks of 'the open land of a man called Munda'.

Under the entry for Brightling we find the minor name of Darwell Hole. As explained, this is from *deor fald*, 'the fold for animals' and not 'deer' as this would not make sense. At Mountfield we find Darwell Furnace Farm, showing not only that this was a farm but also that iron was once smelted, presumably at different times.

Eatenden Wood puts together Old English *ing tun* with a Saxon personal name, this meaning 'the farmstead associated with a man called Ita'. Glottenham has a personal name and Old English *ing ham* giving 'the homestead of the people of Glott'. Hucksteep Wood can be traced to forms showing this was 'the steep ground of Hucc or Huccel'. Lastly a personal name is also found in Woodsale, here is 'the valley of a man called Hod'.

N

Netherfield

Listed as Nedrefelle in the *Domesday* survey of 1086, this is derived from Old English *naeddre feld* and describes 'the open land infested with adders'.

Newhaven

The present name is, as the name itself suggests, very new. Indeed it is not seen until 1587 and is from Old English *niwe haefen* 'the new harbour'. However, this was not founded in the late 16th century as there are records of a settlement here by the 12th century and the place is probably much older. The previous name tells it was the '(place of) the family or followers of a man called Mece', where the Saxon personal name is followed by Old English *inga* and is listed as Mechingas in 1121 and as Mecinges in 1204.

Outside the Engineer public house on Railway Road is an image of the great Victorian engineer Isambard Kingdom Brunel. He built not only railways but the greatest ships of his time, hence the location near the station and the reason a ship is shown in the background on the sign.

This coastal location is echoed in other pub names of Newhaven. The Ark Inn, the Harbourside, the Jolly Boatman, and the Ship Hotel all belong to this category. Another two examples are not what they appear, for while the Flying Fish may seem an obvious reference to the sea it probably came to England as an heraldic image from France. Also the Hope overlooks the ocean and will have originated in a phrase more often seen in pub names, 'hope and anchor' speaking of the hope that one's faith will anchor them through life's troubled waters.

Both the Bridge Inn and Bridge Street leave no doubt this stands adjacent to the Newhaven Swing Bridge. The Prince of Wales is a general reference to those who have held the title, although the attractive green tiled frontage reveals this to be Victorian and thus inspired by the future Edward VII. The Newfield Arms and Newfield Road will have a common origin in exactly what the name tells us, a 'new field'.

Newhaven marks the southern terminus of the Vanguard Way. This route must have the strangest etymology of any long distance path in the land. These 66 miles from East Croydon were marked out to celebrate the 15th anniversary of the founding of the Vanguards Rambling Club in 1965. This group named themselves after having to return from a walk in the guard's van owing to the train being very crowded.

Newick

A name which is easy to see as coming from Old English *niwe wic* and telling us it was 'the new specialised farm', that speciality invariably dairy produce. While 'new' is the literal meaning of *niwe* it should seen as 'newer', for there cannot be a new anything without an earlier example of a *wic*. The name is recorded as Niwicha in 1121.

Both the Royal Oak and the Crown Inn are pub names referring to the monarchy. The latter is a general reference while the former refers to a specific date in history, the 4 September 1651, when Charles II hid among the branches of an oak tree to evade his pursuers.

The Bull on the Green, the addition a reference to its location, was a stopping place for pilgrims *en route* from Winchester to Canterbury in 1510. This is early enough evidence to suggest this is a symbolic name, the bull representing the papacy and the reason edicts from His Holiness are referred to as a papal bull. The coat of arms of that trade does hang outside Bricklayers Arms, showing a connection to the building trade.

Ninfield

Domesday records this name as Nerewelle in 1086 and is seen again as Nimenefeld in 1255. The great survey is a wonderful record of 11th century England, however, the proper names are notoriously inaccurate which makes defining the name difficult when it is the only early form we have, which is often the case. This problem is easy to see, for the surveyors were Norman Frenchmen and spoke a language which belongs to the Latin branch of the Indo-European language group. The Saxons, who were providing the information, spoke a language belonging to the other arm of this ancient language, the very different Germanic tongues. Thus here it makes sense to rely on the later record from the 13th century, itself clearly from Old English *niwe numen feld* and describing 'the newly taken open land'.

On 12 May 1944, prior to the D-Day landings, the troops were paid a visit here by no fewer than four serving prime ministers. The village gates were erected to commemorate the four statesmen: Rt Hon Winston S. Churchill of Great Britain; Rt Hon Mackenzie King of Canada; Rt Hon Field Marshal Jan Christian Smuts of South Africa; and Hon Sir Godfrey M. Huggins of Southern Rhodesia.

Northiam

Two possible Old English origins for this name recorded as Hiham in *Domesday* and as Nordhyam at the end of the 12th century. With the additional *north*, itself

self-explanatory, the original may be *hig hamm* and 'the hemmed-in land where hay is grown' or *heah hamm* 'the high hemmed-in land'.

Barham Cottages is from *bere hamm*, 'the hemmed-in land where barley is grown'. Dadland Shaw began as 'the agricultural land of a man called Dudda', with the later addition of *sceaga* or 'woodland copse'. Dixter is from *dic steort* 'the ditch at the tongue of land'. While Tufton Place was for many years simply 'the *tun* or farmstead of a man called Tucca'.

The name of the Crown and Thistle public house can be dated to 24 March 1603. On that day the House of Tudor's last English monarch, Elizabeth I, died and was replaced by the House of Stuart. James IV of Scotland and James I of England are the same person, differing regnal numbers for each country. Although this unification was entirely through the monarchy, it does represent the first step to the political union signed in 1707, ironically during the reign of the last of the Stuarts, Queen Anne.

Nunningham Stream

Also known locally as the Bells River, although never officially. This stream took its earlier name from Old English *grima broc*, telling us it flowed through 'the meadow with a goblin by a brook'. The present name is an example of back-formation.

Nutley

Recorded as Nutleg in 1249, this is 'the woodland clearing where nut trees grow' and derived from Old English *hnutu leah*. The local is the Nutley Arms.

Offham

This name comes from Old English *woh hamm* and tells of 'the crooked hemmed-in land'. The name is recorded as Wocham at the end of the 11th century.

Standing on the London Road, the Blacksmiths Arms reminds us that once travellers required stabling and maintenance for their horse and not parking. Certainly this establishment will have seen innumerable horses during its long existence, there is written evidence of this place being used by Simon de Montfort prior to the Battle of Lewes in 1264.

Ore

Numerous examples of this place name, including Ore in 1121, Ora in 1125, Oores in 1265, and Orre in 1535. All show an Old English origin from *ora*, which used to mean 'a flat-topped hill'. History shows both the church and the manor house were located at the top of this hill.

Ouse, River

Formerly called the Midewinde, meaning 'the middle winding river', a name preserved where it passes through Lindfield and the Midwyn Bridge. The modern name comes from the place name of Lewes, listed as Aqua de Lewes which was incorrectly understood as Aqua del Ewes or Ouse.

Ovingdean

Listed as Hovingedene in the *Domesday* record of 1086, here is 'the valley of the family or followers of a man called Ufa' where the Saxon personal name is followed by *inga denu*.

P

Patcham

A name found as Piceham in the *Domesday* survey of 1086 and as Peccham around the end of the 11th century. Here is 'the homestead of a man called Paecca', where the Saxon personal name is followed by *ham*.

Brapool Barn tells us it was located at 'the pool near where bracken grows'. The names of Moulsecoombe 'the valley of a man called Mul' and Withdean 'the valley of a man called Wihta' have similar meanings but are derived from the suffixes *cumb* and *denu* respectively.

Locals enjoy a glass of their favourite tipple in the Long Man of Wilmington. This famous chalk figure stands on the steep slope of Windover Hill and measures 227 feet from head to toe. Some consider this to be very ancient, one source claiming a date of 3480 BC, however, this is based on the idea it was to mark the position of the constellation of Orion the Hunter and does not stand up to archaeological study. It is generally accepted this dates from the 16th or 17th centuries, although what it was designed for is unclear.

Another unique pub name in the same village is the Ladies Mile. Traditionally this stands on a stretch of road where Regency belles would parade on their wonderfully groomed horses riding side-saddle while draped in the fashions of the day.

Peacehaven

A very recent name given to a resort created to mark the end of World War One. The place of peace offers a warm welcome in a couple of its pub names. The invitation to please 'do drop in' is found at the Dewdrop Inn, while a place to find friends is the message given by the Good Companions. The Sussex Coaster refers to a trading vessel, although the fact that this lies on the coast road was undoubtedly a factor. Similarly the White Schooner, another reference to an ocean-going vessel, could also be seen as a white building where sherry is served in a glass called a schooner.

Peasmarsh

Found as Pisemerse in the 12th century, this name comes from Old English *pise mersc* and describes 'the marshy ground where peas are grown'.

Barline is a local name derived from Old English *beorg glind*, meaning 'the enclosure at the hill'. From the same language, Dinglesden also features two elements. This time *thengel denu* tells of 'the valley of the prince', although the use of *thengel* was not only used to refer to royalty, originally the term described a son, particularly one who was likely to inherit.

Flackley Ash, the addition comparatively recent and points to an ash tree, has its first element from a Saxon personal name with Old English *leah* and telling of 'the woodland clearing of a man called Flaecca'. Another personal name is seen in Pelsham, here suffixed by *ham* to tell of 'the homestead of a man called Pydel'. A similar arrangement is seen in Tillingham Farm, although here the personal name has two Old English elements. Together with *inga ham* this describes 'the homestead of the family or followers of a man called Tila or Tilli'.

Peacehaven's welcoming sign.

Pubs include the Horse and Cart, a look back to the days when this was how goods were transported and the pub offered refreshment. The Cock Horse was a term applied to the extra horse, a powerful animal, tethered to the front of the team in order to tackle a particularly arduous ascent.

Penhurst

Domesday records this name as Penehest, later it is found as Peneherste in the 12th century. Here a Saxon personal name and Old English *hyrst* tell of 'the wooded hill of a man called Pena'.

Bridgen Hill reminds us this was originally known as 'the swine pasture of a man called Brica'. Frankwell is not difficult to see as 'the spring or stream of a man called Franca', the Saxon personal name suffixed by *wiella*. Pannelridge Wood has few early forms, however, this does not mean we cannot offer a definition. The suffix is certainly *hrycg* and possibly marks a 'place at the ridge of a penny rent'. It was later transferred and used for the name of the wood.

Pett

Records of this name include Ivet in 1086, Pette in 1195, and Putte in 1287. Ignoring the *Domesday* record of Ivet, it being written by Norman Frenchmen, the remainder would reflect a better understanding of Old English, this would come from *pytt* and refer to some '(now lost) pitt or well'.

Local names include Dimsdale, the Saxon personal name suffixed by Old English *dael* to describe 'the valley of a man called Dynne'.

Public houses include the Royal Oak, another referring to Charles II's escape and instantly popular following the Restoration of the Monarchy in 1660. With a near coastal location the name of the Smugglers would readily suggest itself today, although it seems unwise to advertise a distribution centre for contraband on a pub sign.

While place names featuring less than complimentary elements are found everywhere across England, to find such in a pub name is quite rare. Workers in first wood and later stone were lauded for their great skills, these were recognised by the creation of guilds for masons, carpenters, joiners, and shipwrights. All these craftsmen required the materials to be cut and worked into manageable sizes. However, they saw these men, who used a long double-handed saw, as second-rate craftsmen and thus what should have become the sawyers arms is a pub named the Two Sawyers.

Pevensey

Documented as Pefenesea in 947 and as Pevenesel in 1086, this is from a Saxon personal name and Old English *ea* and describing 'the river of a man called Pefen'.

Here is Chilley, from a Saxon personal name with Old English *eg* to describe 'the island of a man called Cilla'. Horse Eye features the elements *hors eg* 'the island where horses are reared'. Clearly neither are islands in the modern sense today, indeed they never were but simply higher and therefore drier ground in marshland. Lampham is derived from 'the *hamm* or hemmed-in land of a man called Lamb'. Wrenham Stream took the name of the bordering land, that name coming from *wren hamm* and referring to 'the hemmed-in land frequented by wrens'.

Public houses here include the obvious location of the Beach Tavern, Bay Hotel, and the Moorings. Predictably the Smugglers is also found near the shoreline. Any example of an oddly coloured animal is an indication of an heraldic image. This includes the most common pub name in the country; the Red Lion shows a link to Scotland.

The Royal Oak and Castle Inn features the second most common name, the Royal Oak, which refers to when Charles II hid in an oak tree to escape the Parliamentarians, and adds a link to the building named by the Pevensey Castle

Hotel and also the Castle. Most often such 'double' pub names show the premises has been known by each at different times. A former use for another building is marked by the name of the Old Mint House, claimed to date from the 14th century, while the Priory Court Hotel is a reminder of former church land.

Piddinghoe

Found as Pidingeho in the 12th century, here the Saxon personal name is suffixed by Old English *inga hoh* and tells of 'the hill spur of land of the family or followers of a man called Pyda'.

Here we find Halcombe Farm; derived from Old English *horh cumb* it tells us this was 'the dirty or muddy valley'.

Playden

Seen as Pleidena in *Domesday*, this name is similar to the previous name and derived from Old English *plega denn* and speaks of 'the woodland pasture where play or sport takes place'.

Saltcote would have been an important place when it was known as 'the salt pan cottages'. Salt was vital to our ancestors who did not have the choice of popping down to the shop if they wanted to stock up on meat for leaner times, or to ensure there was cheese on the menu, or perhaps to browse for leather goods. They had to be made at home and all require salt.

Unlike other necessities such as grain, red meat, vegetables, fish, wool, herbs, and cloth, which could be produced on site, salt was a rare commodity indeed. This made it valuable, indeed there is evidence of how salt was not simply exchanged for high prices but was used as currency. The Roman Empire covered a huge area and, without any standard coinage, salt became the universal currency and thus their soldiers were paid in salt. Indeed the word 'soldier' and 'salary' are both derived from the Latin for 'salt'.

An unusual, but by no means unique, pub name is that of the Peace and Plenty. This name is first known following the cessation of hostilities of the Napoleonic Wars in 1815. The message of calm and abundance is clear; however, the name may be older as the source is undoubtedly Shakespearian. This comes from *Cymbeline* Act 5, Scene 5 when the soothsayer reads a passage telling how Cymbeline's sons shall bring peace and plenty to Britain.

Plumpton

A name found as Plumtone in 1086, as Plumtonam in 1201, and as Plompton in 1279. Here is a name from Old English *plume tun* or 'the farmstead where plum trees grow'.

Locally we find Wales Farm, named from the family of Walter de Westwales, here by 1332.

One pub is the Plough at Plumpton. Found since at least the 16th century, the plough has been used as a pub name to show those who worked the land were welcome within, effectively open to all as few did not depend on the land. As a common name it made sense to add a distinctive element, there can be no clearer message than to add the place name.

From an heraldic device showing a link to either the Plumbers' Company or the Master Mariners, it should be noted the Fountain Inn could simply refer to a nearby spring. The Half Moon Inn is certainly heraldic, although the modern sign depicts a lunar image. Clearly the local racecourse was the idea behind the Winning Post.

Polegate

A name not seen until 1563 where it appears as Powlegate Corner. This name comes from Middle English *poole* and Old English *geat* and describes 'the gate or gap by a pool'.

The Junction pub sign is one of the few remaining signs of the former railway station at Polegate.

Four streets are named after the most prominent family in Polegate; Levett Close, Levett Road, Levett Avenue and Levett Way.

Local place names include that which gave a name to the Berwick Arms, it being from Old English *bere wic* 'the farm specialising in barley'. Other pubs include the stabling once advertised by the Horse and Groom. A more impressive equine lineage is the Thoroughbred. That of the Sussex Ox is not a reference to a particular animal, indeed the place was known as the Royal Oak until the 1970s. This came from the original building which opened as a slaughterhouse fronted by a butcher's shop in the first decade of the 20th century.

The certainly original name of the Dinkum was used by locals well before it was officially adopted by the owners. This dates from World War One when hospitalised Australians passed this way on their daily walk of two miles. As this was within a mile of their base this Aussie expression told how they saw this establishment as a positive factor in their recovery.

No surprise to find both Station Road and the Junction Tavern within a stone's throw of the railway line. Similarly large and very long-lived trees would have suggested themselves as ideal markers for both the Old Oak Inn and the Yew Tree. The Barley Mow advertises the product in a stack of barley, this being a major ingredient in brewing. Showing the nation's official summer sport was played by a team based here is the name of the Cricketers Arms.

Portslade by Sea

Records of this name include Porteslage in *Domesday* and as Portes Ladda at the end of the 11th century. Here Old English *port gelad* combines to give 'the crossing place near the harbour'.

The suggestion that this was named by the Romans is today known to be wrong. While there is evidence of Roman activity here, the idea this place was the port of Novus Pontus written about by Ptolemy in the second century AD is based entirely on the assumption that Drove Road was the Roman road spoken of in this same work. There is an early name of Copperas Gap, copperas being green vitriol which was used extensively in the textile industry. Processing the nodules found in the Sussex greensand here took six years before it could be used in the production of cloth.

Atlingworth Barn features a Saxon personal name and Old English *worth inga* telling of 'the enclosure of the family or followers of a man called Aethling'.

Mill Lane, and the Mill House pub named after it, speak for themselves. The Gardeners Arms began as an alternative to an agricultural name such as the plough or farmer. On land associated with the church, as evidenced by roads named St Leonards Road, St Leonards Avenue, and St Leonards Gardens, is the Blue Anchor. The colour has long been used to represent Christianity, while the anchor stands for the hope that one's faith will serve as an anchor through life, a reference to Hebrews chapter 6, verse 19. A more obvious reference, and this time it does owe its existence to the nearby shoreline, is that of the Harbour View.

The Whistlestop Inn is an imaginative name, one where its proximity to the railway station (and the days of the steam train) is coupled with an invitation to pop in for a quick drink (a whistlestop visit is a brief one). The Cricketers would have started as an advertisement as the establishment had a representative cricket team. 21 October 1805 was an important day in history, many will recognise this as the date the Royal Navy defeated a combined French and Spanish fleet and gave the Battle of Trafalgar public house a name.

The Kings Head may depict the unmistakeable image of King Henry VIII, however, it is easy to see these premises were built in the 20th century not the 16th. The message here is one of patriotism. The Albion public house features the Latin name for Britain, it being derived from the white cliffs which dominate this part of the coastline. The Stanley Arms features the family name of the earls of Derby, who have held a good deal of land in England.

The Victoria Inn is easily seen as a reference to our longest-ever reigning monarch, Queen Victoria, although effectively the pub took the name of Victoria

Road on which it stands. Such patriotism is even more to the fore in the name of the St George Inn, he being the patron saint of England. That the Stags Head is found here is probably an indication the name is heraldic rather than a reference to the hunt. Oak trees are virtually permanent markers in the landscape. Long-lived and easily seen, the Mile Oak Inn in Mile Oak Road both show a name from a marker or mile post.

Preston

A common place name normally found with a second defining element. This name is always derived from Old English *preost tun* and tells of 'the farmstead of the priest' and was recorded as Prestetone in 1086.

R

Ringmer

Listed as Ryngemere in 1276, this is from Old English *hring mere* and describes 'the pool near a circular feature'.

Here we find Chamberlaines, not named after Sir William Waleys directly but from his position as a bailiff of the Archbishop of Canterbury. Delves House is the only remaining evidence of a name which features an element still used meaning 'to seek or dig out'. The house took an existing name, itself revealing this was the site of a 'digging or quarry'. In the case of Wellingham, *wella inga hamm* come together to speak of 'the hemmed-in land of the dwellers by the stream'.

The Old Ship is a 17th-century inn located, in their own words, '...in the heart of the Sussex countryside' which seems an odd place to find any ship. The majority of supposed 'ship' names found inland are a corruption of Old English *sceap* meaning 'sheep', inns which were a vital part of the distribution network for wool.

To some degree the Cock Inn has a similar background, for the name of a male bird has no connection with the suggested etymology while it does share a link to old transport methods. Here the 'cock', a name which certainly has been in use since 1739, is a strong horse attached to the front of the team pulling the waggon. Used to negotiate particularly tough sections, such would have proven highly useful on this road.

The Green Man is an image most often depicting the woodsman, an important member of the community in the 16th century when the name first became popular. The Anchor Inn shows a connection to the church, this being taken from the bible when St Paul speaks of one's faith being the anchor through life's storms.

Three characters suggest themselves as potential unique place names which are pertinent only to Ringmer. Naturalist Gilbert White is associated with one of the village's most famous former residents. Rebecca Snooke, White's aunt, lived in the village and was presented with a female tortoise by her nephew in 1780. This female tortoise was named Timothy, it is still difficult to sex tortoises, and had free run of Rebecca's garden. Gilbert White died in 1793 and, one year later, Timothy perished.

Ripe

Domesday's record from 1086 is exactly as it appears today. This comes from Old English *rip* and refers to the '(place at) the strip of land'.

Locally we find Eckington Corner, derived from a Saxon personal name and Old English *inga tun* and referring to 'the farmstead of the family or followers of a man called Heaha'. The use of Deanland is discovered when defining 'the pasture land where swine are reared'.

Locals using the Lamb Inn may well be unaware this has nothing to do with sheep of any kind. Here the reference is religious and speaks of Christ who is described as the 'Lamb of God' in the book of Hebrews. Further evidence is offered by the road these premises are located on, Church Lane.

Robertsbridge

Found as Pons Roberti in 1176 and as Robartesbregge in 1445, this name comes from Robert de St Martin who founded the abbey here in the 12th century.

We also find the hamlet of John's Cross here, it named so for it was a meeting point for those heading for the Crusades, who travelled under the banner of John the Baptist. Said banner featured a cross, hence the name of the John's Cross Inn. Similarly the hamlet of Staplecross gave a name to the Cross Inn, the place name is derived from Old English *stapol* and tells of 'the crossroads marked by a post'.

Other pubs here include the White Hart, which first suggested itself as a pub name when Richard II came to the throne in 1377 as it is the most obvious device in his coat of arms. However, thereafter it remained popular owing to it being used as the generic term for any pub, much as vacuum cleaners are referred to as Hoovers today.

The Castle is named after nearby Bodiam Castle, a 14th-century moated fortification which helped to defend England against French invasion during the Hundred Years War. Built at the same time was the Seven Stars public house, the origin of which is unclear but may have been brought to England by the De Fontabus family, who were certainly here by the late 12th century.

During the 1850s the lords of the manor of Robertsbridge were the Allfrey family, who featured a flightless bird in their coat of arms, hence the name of the Ostrich Hotel. Another bird, the Curlew, gave its name to the premises which began as a coaching inn.

Rodmell

Seen as Redmelle in 1086 and as Radmelse in 1202, this is from Old English *read mylde* and tells of the '(place by) the red soil'.

Northease Farm began as *north hese* and described 'the northern land covered by brushwood'.

Built some four centuries ago, the Abergavenny Arms was named after Lord Abergavenny, a title held by the Neville Family. Note it spent a few years as the Holly Inn but reverted to its original name in 1985.

The village is the location of Monk's House. From 1920 this was the home of author Virginia Woolf until, on 28 March 1941, she left her home for the final time and walked through the fields to the River Ouse where she drowned herself.

Rotherfield

A name meaning 'the open land where cattle graze', this is derived from Old English *hryther feld* and is recorded as Hyrtheranfeld around the end of the ninth century and as Reredfelle in *Domesday*. The River Rother is an example of back-formation, named from Rotherfield.

Bletchingley features Old English *inga leah* with a Saxon personal name to speak of 'the woodland clearing of the family or followers of a man called Blaecca'. The Forstal is a late Middle English term describing 'the paddock near a farmhouse'. Inchreed suggests something rather different from the original 'increeping', where the boundary of the cleared land is thought to be slowly advancing. Orznash is an unusual English name, although the origin is Saxon in 'the stubble land of a man called Osa'. Rumsden Farm was established on the land known for its 'spacious swine pasture'.

There are two public houses here, the Kings Arms shows support for the monarch, while the Catts Inn takes its name from the local squire, Mr Catt owning these premises from around the middle of the 18th century.

Rottingdean

Found as Rotingedene in the *Domesday* survey of 1086, here is a Saxon personal name and Old English *inga denu* which describes 'the valley of the family or followers of a man called Rota'.

Minor names here feature the same suffix, once both were separate settlements. What began as 'the valley of a man called Beald' is now known as Balsdean, while *ruh denu* or 'the rough valley' referred to the overgrown area which is now Roedean and the name of probably the most famous school for girls in the country.

Public houses here begin with the Queen Victoria, the last British ruler of the House of Hanover. Originating in Germany, the Hanoverian device is represented on the sign outside the White Horse Hotel. Similarly the Black Horse is probably derived from a family crest, although the image is so common it is impossible to say which coat of arms it represents, while the idea that this remembers a favourite animal cannot be ruled out completely. What is certain is that this animal will not have pulled the agricultural tool which gave a name to the Plough Inn, for this name was coined to attract farm workers at a time when the plough would be drawn by oxen.

Rye

Listed as Ria in 1130, this comes from Middle English *atter* and Old English *ieg* and describes the '(place) at the dry ground in a marsh'.

In the main street names tend to originate from a later time than place names. For many years they were overlooked as a source of historical information and yet historians and archaeologists are increasingly seeing their worth. Not only do they remember the rich and famous but, as we shall see, the tradesman or his wares, and the daily activities associated with the area.

Many place names are merely indicators of location, even those featuring a personal name have a second element describing the area. To some degree the same is true of road and street names. There are many simply referring to where that route would take a traveller, particularly important when the vast majority of the population were illiterate. Hence we find East Street, which does still exist,

Market Street, Rye.

and also West Street, although previously known as Middle Street as it was at the very centre of the town, and earlier still as Mermaid Street, a link to the public house, as in the case of Lion Street and the former Red Lion public house.

Other name changes include High Street, named for being the most important street in the town, which had earlier been known by other names including Lower Street, itself confirmation of it not being at the highest point on the hill. At other times it was known as Mint Street, for this was where coins were minted, and in the 16th century as Long Street, not for its length but from the Longe family who lived here. What is now Market Road, itself self-explanatory, was previously known as Jarrett's Yard after the man who owned this part of the town.

Despite the name of Cinque Ports Street, Rye was never truly one of the five 'Cinque Ports' but was, along with 'Wincheslea', an 'Antient Town'. Such additions were necessary when former ports were silted up, such as in the case of New Romney and Sandwich. Together these formed a chain of defensive locations along the coast of Sussex and Kent. Together with seven 'Limbs' and 23 'Connected Towns' they were charged with defending the realm by a Royal Charter of 1155. Justifiably proud of this status the term is maintained, albeit today only in ceremonial matters.

Now known as The Needles, although nobody ever bothered to note why the name was chosen, this thoroughfare was earlier known as Vennalls Passage. The Vennalls family were prominent locally right up to the 20th century. Records differ as to even earlier names, hence we must assume both were applicable at some time. Either this was Carpenter's Lane, perhaps a trade name but more likely a family name, or it was Coggles Lane, itself referring to the 'cobbled' surface.

No surprise to find Watchbell Street and Watchbell Lane have a common origin in the watchbell tower. This was erected shortly after the attack by the

Jarretts Close, Rye.

Cinque Ports public house in Rye.

French in 1377, when the bells of the church were stolen. This may seem an odd target for thieves today, however, we must remember these were the sole method of alerting the local population the town had been invaded, effectively a 14th-century version of cutting the burglar alarm. Ye Olde Bell Inn shares this origin.

Other local names include Cadborough, Old English for 'the hill where goats are raised'. Holmdale refers to the vegetation in 'the valley where holly grows'.

Pub names begin with the William the Conqueror which, in this part of the world, is a most appropriate and predictable choice. At the Kings Head the image is clearly that of George III, whose reign of 60 years was marked by mental illness meaning his son, the future George IV, acted as Prince Regent. At the Queens Head we see an image of Elizabeth I, while the Crown Inn is a general reference to the monarchy.

The Union Inn has a painting on the outside wall of a rose, a thistle and a shamrock. Discovered during refurbishment work it clearly refers to the union

Cinque Ports pub sign in Rye.

Rye Tower.

The old Water Works pump house in Tower Street, Rye.

of the three crowns of England (the rose), Scotland (the thistle) and Ireland (the shamrock) at the accession of James I of England and VI of Scotland. The Red Lion became popular at this time too and is now the most common pub name in England although, ironically, it represents Scotland.

Strands Bar is named for its location on the Strand. Aptly named for being on Rye Hill is the Top O The Hill. The Standard occupies the building still known as the Mint, which points to this being derived from the quality control methods used to ensure the correct proportions of metals were used in manufacture. Once a warehouse used by excise men to hold contraband taken from smugglers, the Ship may well contain timbers from vessels taken by the long arm of the law.

The Globe was a simple image conveying the message that this establishment welcomed all. Hare and Hounds is a reminder of hare coursing, a blood sport banned in 2005. A menu was in the mind when naming the Rainbow Trout. Named for the dukes of Bedford, probable landowners, is the Bedford Arms. The Ypres Castle Inn is a bit of an exaggeration, for this is named for the nearby Ypres Tower. The unusually named Rumples Inn features a sign showing the eponymous character from the childrens' story named Rumplestiltskin.

The Pipe Makers Arms features an attractive image carved in the apex and painted colourfully to show the importance of this skill. The Inkerman Arms remembers the Battle of Inkerman, named after the town in the Crimea which was the site of a terrific battle on 5 November 1854. Both the defeated Russians and the victorious British and French allies lost great numbers of men.

The Mermaid Inn dates from around 1420, although the cellars existed in 1156 and may be even older. It was one of the many inns of this coastline frequented by the notorious Hawkhurst Gang, smugglers who were active during the 1730s and 1740s and discussed under the entry for Sedlescombe. Here the memory of this gang may still live on in the form of some uninvited out-of-this world guests.

The James Room is said to be haunted by a grey lady (other reports say she is dressed in white) who is seen seated in a chair. Clothes left on this chair overnight by guests have been found to be wet the next morning. Nearby the Nutcracker Suite plays host to a white lady who crosses the room, pausing at the foot of the bed. Another roaming phantom disturbs guests in the Fleur de Lys room by passing straight through the wall into the *en suite* bathroom.

When we arrive at the Elizabethan room we find the first of the stories continuing to link this place with the smugglers. A maid is said to be seen here, this being the room where she was murdered. The girlfriend of one of a gang, she was killed by his colleagues as they considered she knew more than enough to expose them. The Hawkhurst Suite is named after this gang, although it is not clear if the 'gentlemen in old fashioned dress' is a former member.

In the Kingsmill Room a chair would rock in the middle of the night in an icy cold room where nobody other than the guests were present. It was held to be haunted by a woman who was the wife of gang founder member George Gray. This room was once held to be home to Thomas Kingsmill, hence the name, another of the Hawkhurst mob.

S

St Ann Without

It hardly seems necessary to state this has a religious origin. However, there is a little more to this name than a church dedicated to St Ann, indeed even the modern spelling of the saint's name is erroneous. Taking all the clues from early forms into account we arrive at a definition for St Ann Without of 'the border stone of the boundary against the chancel of St Mary and also St Annes'.

Locally Ashcombe House was built at a place already known for 'the *cumb* or valley marked by the ash tree'. Houndean Bottom, may refer to 'the valley of the hounds' or, should the first element be a personal name, 'the valley of a man called Hunda'.

St John Without

Despite the similarity with the previous name, records show this has a simpler origin, although only just. Listed in the 12th century as Ecclesia sci Johannis sub castro, this tells of 'the ancient parish church of St John' being only just within the parish, indeed rather extraordinarily it seems most of it officially lay outside the parish boundary.

Local names include Allington Farm, where a Saxon personal name is followed by Old English *in tun* to tell of 'the farmstead associated with a man called Aella'. Note this is not *inga* but *ing*, while the two are very similar there is a very important difference in meaning. Had this been *inga* it would have told of 'the farmstead of the family or followers of a man called Aella' which reveals the man himself was never here and thus probably named posthumously.

Kandport is certainly a corruption, early records show this is not from *land port*. However, it is unclear if the first element is *lam*, and thus 'the place with a market known for lambs', or *lang*, giving 'the long place with a market'.

St Leonards

Recorded as Villa de Sancto Leonardo juxta Hasting in 1288, literally 'the manor of St Leonard near Hastings', this is named from the dedication of the church here. However, that church will not be found today; it was destroyed when the sea encroached in the 15th century.

The Royal Hotel either shows this once had a royal visitor or deemed itself fit for such. The Duke and the Clarence is named after the Duke of Clarence, Prince Albert Victor, who was a son of Queen Victoria. Both parents are represented too, in the shape of the Royal Albert and the Victoria Inn. The Prince of Wales may be a general reference to the title held by the heir to the throne, similarly the Crown House indicates a link to the ruling house.

The Duke is named after the Duke of Wellington, one of our nation's most celebrated soldiers who also served his country as a politician. The Bulverhythe takes a local place name, one meaning 'the landing place of the dwellers in the town'. The Fox is most often chosen for being an easily recognised image. When naming the North Star Inn the ocean was in mind, it being the point of reference for navigation in the northern hemisphere. Yet the Comet is not an astronomical reference; this was the name of a famous stagecoach and shows this was a stop on the route.

As a pointer to either the Worshipful Company of Bakers of the Brewers' Company, the name of the Wheatsheaf has retained its popularity. An image used by many, including Edward III and Richard III, has given a name to the Rising Sun. While the Bull might represent a prized animal, more often it will represent an image from one of the many coats of arms which includes this powerful image.

We are naturally reluctant to change and find comfort in past experiences, and nostalgia is the message in the name of the Old England and a suggestion to sample what can be found within. Such an invitation is also offered in the name of the Welcome Stranger. The Railway is also a welcoming name, offering refreshment from times when this was the main mode of travel. Another mode of travel is seen in the Nags Head. Once a nag was not a derogatory term for a horse but simply referred to a stocky mount which could be hired for a journey.

The Harrow Inn features an image of the agricultural tool used to till the soil after ploughing and/or sowing. A far too rare double-sided sign outside the Bo-Peep shows the nursery rhyme character on one side, although the true origin is on the reverse where smugglers engaged in nefarious activities hidden from the excise men. This is not without basis in fact for, in 1828, the long arm of the law reached out to capture the criminals and a bloody battle ensued. Wishing Tree Lane North has the Wishing Tree public house, both recalling a snippet of folklore.

In times when houses would brew their own ales a reliable source of fresh water was vital. We must assume that source either dried up or was unreliable in the case of the Dripping Spring. Travellers were also enticed by the promise of hospitality for their mount as well as themselves, hence the name of the Horse and Groom. Advertising is also found in the name of the Marina Fountain Inn, both elements refer to the sea, as the fountain is a device found in the coat of arms of the Master Mariners.

The Hollington Oak is a pub where the name points to a large tree which acted as a permanent marker for the premises, at least effectively permanent as the oak could live 10 times that of the human life span. That it is described as the Hollington Oak also shows it was used as a marker for a route to neighbouring Hollington. While the modern route is not a straight line, extending the line of Wishing Tree Lane makes for a very direct path. Note the name of Wishing Tree Lane, which likely predates the name of the pub and is an indication this was seen in some spiritual light.

Salehurst

Listed as Salhert in *Domesday* and as Salhirst in the early 13th century, this is from Old English *salh hyrst* and describes 'the wooded hill where sallow trees grow'.

Local names include Bernhurst, a common Saxon name followed by *hyrst* giving 'the wooded hill of a man called Beorna'. Bugsell has a similar origin, here the meaning is 'the hill of a man called Buck', while Wigsell repeats the pattern in 'the hill of a man called Wicga'. Iridge Place is not hard to see as 'the ridge of land marked by yew trees' from Old English *iw hrycg*.

Seaford

A name which means 'the ford by the sea' from Old English *sae ford*. The name is first found in the 12th century as Saforde, where the travellers crossed the River Ouse which flowed into the sea here until the 16th century.

Chyngton Farm is derived from a Saxon place name describing 'the farmstead associated with a man called Cintin', the personal name followed by Old English *ing tun*.

Pubs of Seaford include the Golden Galleon, a reminder of this region's past when smugglers landed contraband, for this was once a prosperous port. A constant battle fought against the silting up of the harbour kept the sea open

St Leonard's Church at the oddly named Place Lane, Seaford.

and maintained the local economy. Yet the balance was tipped during a 200-year period. From the middle of the 14th century the town was raided and burned numerous times by the French and times of prosperity were over.

The Bay Tree is a new addition to the pubs of Seaford. It uses the image of the tree whose leaves are used in cooking and also hints at the nearby coastline, the Shore has similar origins. The Beachcomber is a direct reference to the shoreline,

Golden Galleon public house sign near Seaford

a beachcomber being an archaic term for a long wave, later adapted to describe Pacific Islanders who scoured the beaches in search of items for food or building materials. Today what they find is the hospitality offered by the pub.

The Cinque Ports is a reminder of the five original coastal towns created by a Royal Charter of 1155. The name is derived from the French *cinq* meaning 'five' but always pronounced as 'sink'. The ports were charged with maintaining ships in a state of readiness for the defence of the realm. The Seven Sisters is a name given to the nearby coastal features, the remnants of seven valleys eroded by rivers flowing in millennia before the English Channel existed and Britain was still attached to the Continent.

Inn signs began as advertising, invitations to sample drink, food or a bed for the night. However, it made no sense to have every inn sign advertising the same delights and other factors were introduced, location, ownership, associated trades, targeted customers. From the 16th century one of the most common pub names was the Plough, an invitation to those who worked the land to take refreshment there, and almost everyone worked the land in those days.

In Seaford the plough name continues to attract custom; here the name is seen as the Old Plough. A modern version targets the white collar workers in the Office Bar. To some degree the same is true of the Old Boot, coming from an expression this tells us this place claims to be resilient, reliable.

Seven Sisters Country Park, near Seaford.

Nobility is always a favourite subject when choosing a name and there is no higher rank than the monarch, here represented by the Crown. The Wellington Hotel recalls the soldier whose most famous victory was against Napoleon at Waterloo, however, Arthur Wellesley, Duke of Wellington was also a leading politician in peace time.

Sedlescombe

Records of this name include Selescombe in *Domesday* and as Sedelescumbe in the early 13th century. This is from Old English *sedl cumb* and describes 'the valley with a dwelling'.

Chittlebirch Farm takes a Saxon name and adds Old English *birce*, a name meaning 'the birch tree of a man called Cetol'. Durhamford has three Old English elements, *deor hamm ford* speaking of 'the ford at the hemmed-in land frequented by deer'.

The Queens Head can trace its history back to the 14th century although, standing on a Roman road, it may well be much, much older. Its name can be traced to the reign of Elizabeth I, when the monarch stayed at this inn. To mark this joyous moment in the village history the locals planted an oak tree on the village green. It still flourishes in the 21st century.

In the cellars are signs of the smugglers' tunnel. Long bricked up, it is a reminder of a time when the notorious Hawkhurst gang brought their particular historical era here. For 15 years from 1735 this was a major operation which began in Kent but spread along the coast as far as Poole in Dorset. It was claimed they could muster at least 500 men for a smuggling run within the hour. The so-called Battle of Goudhurst, a bloody shoot-out with excise men, brought their nefarious careers to an abrupt end.

Selmeston

Seen as Sielmestone in *Domesday*, this is 'the farmstead of a man called Sigehelm', where the Saxon personal name is followed by Old English *tun*.

Ludlay puts together a Saxon personal name and the suffix *leah* to tell us this was once 'the woodland clearing of a man called Leofgyth'. Sherrington also features a Saxon name, here suffixed by *inga tun* and referring to 'the farmstead of the family or followers of a man called Seira'.

Sheffield Green

A name recorded as Sifells in 1086 and as Shipfeud in 1272, this comes from Old English *sceap feld* and describes 'the open land where sheep graze'.

Shoreham by Sea

Found as Sorham in 1073 and as Soreham in 1086, this name comes from Old English *scora ham* and describes 'the homestead by a steep slope'. The addition of 'by Sea' was not seen until the Victorians made seaside holidays popular. Old Shoreham refers to that part of the town built before the arrival of the Normans.

Erringham Farm comes from Old English *inga ham* with a Saxon personal name referring to this as 'the homestead of the family or followers of a man called Erra'.

Southease

A name derived from Old English *suth haese* or 'the southern land overgrown with brushwood', this is recorded as Sueise in 966 and as Suesse in 1086.

The Church of St Peter dates from the 12th century. It is one of only three surviving churches in East or West Sussex with a round tower.

Southover

A name found in the 12th century as Suthoure and later as Suthenore. Here is 'the southern bank' from Old English *sud ofer*, a name referring to its location on the southern bank of the Winterbourne stream.

Local names include Rise Farm and Rise Barn, both occupying an area of land which rose higher than the marshland and was thus much drier. St Pancras Lane was named for the nearby monastery.

Spithurst

Here Middle English *split* combines with Old English *hyrst* to tell of 'the wooded hill at the opening or gap'. The earliest record of this name dates from 1296 as Splyherst.

Stanmer

Recorded as Stanmere in 765, this is easily seen as Old English *stan mere* describing 'the stony pool'.

Streat

A simple enough name to define for it tells us this village stands on a Roman road. However, the origin is not Latin, the Romans did almost nothing when it came to naming places anywhere in their vast empire, but this comes from the Old English *straet*.

Sussex

The county name is first found in a late ninth century document as Suth Seaxe, while *Domesday* refers to it as Sudsexe. Both of these early forms clearly represent Old English *suth Seaxe* and tell us of the '(territory) of the southern Saxons', relative to that of the west Saxons in what was Wessex, the east Saxons of Essex, and middle Saxons of Middlesex.

Tarring Neville

Found as Toringes in 1086 and as Thoring Nevell in 1339, the basic name has two possible Old English origins. Should the first element be a Saxon personal name, this would be suffixed by *inga* and give the '(place of) the family or followers of a man called Teorra'. However, this could represent *torr ingas* and 'the dwellers of the rocky hill'. The addition is manorial, the de Neville family were here by the 13th century.

Telscombe

Recorded as Titelescumbe in 946, here is 'the valley of a man called Titel' and is derived from a Saxon personal name and Old English *cumb*.

The Badgers Watch public house tells us it was a place where badgers were seen and monitored. The Telscombe Tavern shows its location, not to locals but outsiders.

Ticehurst

From Old English *ticcen hyrst* comes 'the wooded hill of the young goats'. First seen in a document of 1248 as Tycheherst.

Telscombe Cliffs.

Battenhurst Farm takes a Saxon personal name and adds Old English *ersc*, together these refer to this as 'the stubble field of a man called Beta'. Clearly this is not a compliment and suggests the man was not a good farmer, at least not considered so by his neighbours. Collington Wood takes an existing place name, the wood probably known by a different name before taking that of 'the farmstead associated with a man called Cola', the personal name suffixed by *ing tun*. Witherden recalls 'the swine pasture of a man called Wither'.

Boarzell is not difficult to see as 'the hill frequented by wild boar'. Flimwell speaks of 'the spring of the fugitive', although it would be wrong to take this literally and is likely another derogatory name. Quedley reveals itself as the site of some unknown superstition, for this refers to the *cwede leh*, Old English for 'the evil or wicked woodland clearing'. London Barn Farm has no connection with the capital city, this is a corruption of *lind denu* 'the valley of the lime trees'.

Shaver's Green is derived from *scylfing* meaning 'see saw'. Not an early

Smugglers Rest public house, Telscombe Cliffs.

example of a playground, here used as an adjective, the reference to oscillations are unclear. Local industry is remembered by the name of Hammerden, these being the forge hammers used by metal workers.

The Cherry Tree Inn would probably have begun as a marker, when in full blossom in the spring it would have made for a most obvious indication of these premises. An heraldic origin cannot be ruled out, although it is difficult to see who this would represent here. This is not true in the case of the Chequers Inn, an image which began in Roman times to indicate the distraction of a boardgame and developed to become the Exchequer, the financial authority in the land.

The Duke of York was named after the eponymous nursery rhyme character. Frederick Augustus, Duke of York was the second son of George III and commander of the army in Flanders at the end of the 18th century. However, the rhyme is somewhat inaccurate for the 'Grand Old Duke of York' was just 31 at the time of the conflict, although he was undoubtedly grand. Neither did he march men up and down hills, for there are no hills in this part of the world, while he commanded more than the 10,000 men, in fact three times that number.

Uckfield

Listed as Uckefeld in 1220, here is 'the open land of a man called Ucca' where the Saxon personal name is suffixed by Old English *feld*. Here we find a dialect word in Ringles Cross, this speaking of 'a little ring' and a reference to some local feature. This was soon seen as an excellent name for the local pub.

Other pub names include the Highlands Inn, which must have been named to show a link to that part of Scotland. The image of dancers forming intricate patterns on the village green is brought to mind when hearing the name of the Maypole Inn. The Foresters Arms is a sign this was a meeting place for the Ancient Order of Foresters, a friendly society with such 'courts' across Britain and the United States.

The Maiden's Head is probably heraldic, possibly a reference to the dukes of Buckingham but more likely representing the Mercers' Company. Maybe the Firemans Arms is a pointer to this being associated with a landlord whose earlier career saw him fighting fires. The William IV is named after the so-called 'Sailor King', whose naval career lasted some 50 years while he reigned for just seven. A bird which makes for an attractive sign and also chosen for an heraldic device of many families for the same reason.

The New Inn is a common name which shows this was not the first pub built here. Yet just by looking at this place we can see this is no longer new and thus perhaps 'the newer inn' would have been a better name. The Alma is named after the first significant conflict of the Crimean War, fought on 20 September 1854. Trade names are popular as pub names, perhaps a former career inspired the naming of the Brickmakers Arms.

When hearing the phrase Cock and Bull it is not the name of a pub which first comes to mind. Such speaks of a 'cock and bull story', that is one with little or no truth in it. As a phrase it is derived from such stories as those of Aesop where cocks speak of morals and bull debate, in use by the 17th century. As a pub name it may represent a comment by an early landlord on an issue of the day, or a combination of elements taken from relevant coats of arms.

A better known origin is the name of the Piltdown Man public house. In 1908 the jawbone and skull of an anthropoid were uncovered from a gravel pit at Piltdown. Four years later Charles Dawson hailed it as the 'missing link' between apes and man, and it was given the Latin name of *Eoanthropus dawsoni*. It proved controversial for more than four decades until exposed as a fraud in 1953 as the jawbone of an orang-u-tan and a modern human skull.

Udimore

Found in *Domesday* as Dodimere and in the 12th century as Odumer, this is derived from Old English *wudig mere* or 'the woody pond'.

Billingham is a local name with its origins in a Saxon personal name and Old English *ham* giving 'the homestead of a man called Billa'. The modern form would appear to show this to be from *ing ham* or *inga ham*, yet the early forms reveal this to be a modern development and has no etymological value. Float Farm does have a link to water, however, this has nothing to do with floating, this term warns this is 'deep water'.

V

Vine's Cross

A comparatively late name which simply refers to the crossroads here, the land being associated with the Vyne family by the 16th century.

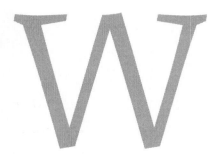

Wadhurst

Documented as Wadehurst in 1253, here a Saxon personal name and Old English *hyrst* refers to 'wooded hill of a man called Wada'.

Early Farm is derived from *earn leah*, the 'woodland clearing frequented by eagles'. What began as 'the swine pasture of a man called Flota' is now seen as Flattenden. Riseden features the same suffix, here giving the meaning of 'the swine pasture overgrown with brushwood'. Any settlement needs a source of water, that being 'the stream of a man called Waenna' and here it only exists today in the name of Wenbans Farm.

Public houses here begin with the Red Lion, the most common name in the country and one which represents Scotland. The Bull Inn is probably another symbolic name, this powerful image chosen by many families. As a pub name the White Hart began in the 14th century, coinciding with the reign of Richard II who used this image in his coat of arms. The image found at the Greyhound represents the dukes of Newcastle, one of the largest landholders in the country.

The Pett Pub, the actual name of the place, takes a nearby place name, one discussed under its own entry as coming from 'the pit or well'. The Best Beech

Inn sends two messages, that this establishment is marked by a large beech tree and also claims it is the best of the pubs here.

Waldron

Found in *Domesday* as Waldrene, here is 'the house in the forest' and is derived from Old English *weald aern*.

Clearhedge Wood gets its name from 'the ridge where clover grows'. Dern Wood is derived from *dierne wudu*, a name referring to this as 'the hidden woodland'. Three elements are found in Possingworth, a Saxon personal name and Old English *inga worth* to tell of 'the enclosure of the family or followers of a man called Posa'.

Warbleton

Domesday lists this name as Warborgetone, here the personal name is followed by Old English *tun* and describes 'the farmstead of a woman called Waerburh'. Female names are likely more common, the problem is identifying them. It is difficult enough to be sure of names, for example we would be unlikely to see the difference between the Saxon equivalents of Micky, Mikey, Michael, Mitchell, Michelle and Michaela. Almost always, as here, the only way to recognise a female personal name is when she is documented as such.

Hereabouts we find Bucksteep, describing itself as 'the place overgrown with beech trees'. Rigsford features the dialect *wrig* with the ageless *ford* to refer to 'the ford marked by willow trees'. Tweazle Wood is an odd-sounding name, one describing 'the wood at the two streams', these two do join here.

Wartling

Found as Werlinges in *Domesday* and as Wertlingis in the 12th century. Here a Saxon personal name and Old English *inga* describes the '(place of) the family or followers of a man called Wyrtel'.

Here is Boreham Street, a road which probably ran past, rather than to, 'the enclosure for boars'. Cowden is derived from Old English *cu denn*, this being 'the woodland pasture for cows'. A Saxon personal name, here followed by *ham*, gives 'the homestead of a man called Hocca', today known as Hockham.

Weald, The

A region documented numerous times in historical documents. Records include Andred in 755 and Andredsweald in 1018, these records showing it was originally known as 'the *weald* of a man called Andred'. The personal name is also seen in Andredesceaster, a Romano-British stronghold recorded when destroyed in 491 by Aella and Cissa. Old English *weald* refers to 'high forested land now cleared'.

Westfield

Records of this name include Westwelle in *Domesday* and as Westefelde early in the 12th century. Derived from Old English *west feld* and describes 'the westerly open land'.

Local names include Crowham, an Old English reference to 'the enclosure where saffron grows'. Pattleton's Farm began life as 'the farmstead of the people of Pietel'.

Two pubs here, the Plough Inn being of the oldest names and an invitation that this place opened its doors to all, including those who worked the land which, at the time, was the vast majority of the population. The New Inn tells us it was not the first use for this establishment, as writing on the sign of the building tells us this was once the old courthouse.

Westham

A name which represents Old English *west hamm* and tells of 'the western hemmed-in land'. The earliest record dates from 1222 exactly as it appears today.

Friday Street is a local term describing a small collection of houses. The reasons are unclear, although three possible explanations should be considered: Friday is a surname; fish may be the connection, it being the traditional food eaten on that day; and the most likely is it being considered the unluckiest day of the week.

From Old English *dic tun* comes Dittons meaning 'the farmstead of or near a ditch'. The first element of Drockmill Hill is Old English *throcc*, together these refer to 'the hill named from the mill by the ditch or drain'. Glynleigh describes 'the woodland clearing near an enclosure'. A Saxon personal name and Old English *hamm* describe 'the hemmed-in land of a man called Haneca', today known as Hankham. Peelings adds *ing* to the personal name, giving the '(place) of the family or followers of a man called Pydel'. Langney is also Old English, *lang eg* telling of 'the long island', although that 'island' is really dry ground in an area of marsh.

Stone Cross, itself a reminder of an old boundary marker, is home to a very modern windmill. This Grade II listed building operated for a very short period indeed, the last windmill to be built in this part of England was built in 1876 and ended its working life in 1937. Thereafter it began to deteriorate but has now been refurbished and is open to the public.

Westmeston

Documented as Westmaestun in the eighth century and as Wesmestun in *Domesday*, here the name comes from Old English *westmest tun* and refers to 'the most westerly farmstead'. With almost all place names being coined by neighbours, to the inhabitants it was simply 'home' or 'our place'; we can deduce from this that this was named by a settlement east of here.

Novington Manor takes the name of the area where it was built, itself derived from a Saxon personal name with *atten inga tun* which describes its position 'at the farmstead of the family or followers of a man called Offa'.

Whatlington

Seen as Watlingetone in 1086, here a Saxon personal name and Old English *ing tun* tells of 'the farmstead associated with a man called Hwaetel'.

Poppinghole is a local name from *healh* and a Saxon personal name. Here we have 'the nook of land of a man called Poppa'.

The local is the Royal Oak, one of many pubs of this name recalling the flight of Charles II. He hid in an oak tree near Shifnal in Shropshire to escape the Parliamentarians, the name becoming instantly popular following the Restoration in 1660. This name is found a lot on the southeast coast, miles from the incident but within miles of where the King embarked for the safety of the Continent.

Willingdon

Recorded as Willendone in 1086, the *Domesday* record shows this to be a Saxon personal name and Old English *dun* and describes 'the hill of a man called Willa'.

Other names here include Hydneye, a Saxon name describing 'the well-watered land of a man called Hidda'. From the same era comes Ratton, speaking of 'the *tun* or farmstead of a man called Raeda', and what began as 'the camp of a man called Totta' is now known as Tas Combe.

Followers of football, particular those with an interest in the sport north of the border, will recognise the name of Hampden Park. The Willingdon version is not the huge stadium providing a neutral venue for a showpiece cup final and also a suitable home for the national team. However, both share an origin in the name of Viscount Hampden, the grandfather of landowner Lord Willingdon.

Formerly known as Willingdon Halt, Hampden Park Railway Station occupies a unique location in the country's rail network. The East Coastway Line brings passengers here and on to Eastbourne along what was once a branch line completed by another line through Stone Cross, this forming a triangle back to the main line. However, the Stone Cross line was closed and the track lifted. Hence the trains now stop here *en route* to Eastbourne and also have the opportunity to stop a second time on the way back, although not all trains do so.

Pubs here include the Red Lion, a name derived from an emblem representing Scotland. It came to Scotland from an illegitimate line known by the surname Beaufort fathered by John of Gaunt, the most powerful man in England in the 14th century and whose coat of arms included a red lion. This line of the nobility was eventually legitimized by a decree, with the proviso they had no claims on the English throne. Yet they were crowned in Scotland from 1437 and thus, from 1603, also England when the two countries were ruled by the House of Stuart. Hence the image of the Red Lion came to Scotland from John of Gaunt and back to England 200 years later.

The Wheatsheaf is also from symbolism, this being found in the arms of both the Worshipful Company of Bakers and the Brewers' Company. While the latter would seem the more obvious the former is more likely as the publican would often offer his services as both brewer and baker to the small community. The British Queen is a modern name referring to one of the most famous women in history, the leader of the Iceni tribe who was once referred to as Boadicea but now more often said to have been Boudica. Her exploits in leading an uprising against the Romans are the stuff of legends and have resulted in stories of her destroying Colchester and London, certainly true, and that she was buried under what is now King's Cross station, highly improbable.

Wilmington

Given as Wilminte in 1086 and as Wilminton in 1189, here the Saxon personal name and Old English *ing tun* describe 'the farmstead of a man called Wighelm or Wilhelm'.

Endlewick is not of Old English origin, indeed we know almost exactly when this name came about for there is documentary evidence from the reign of Henry VIII (1509-47) to speak of the '11 specialised farm rents' levied here. Apart from his many wives, Henry is remembered for the Dissolution of the Monasteries, thus there is a certain irony on Monkyn Pin Farm speaking of 'the enclosure of the monks'.

The local is the Giant's Rest, a pub with an amusing image of the soles of two feet of a large individual who is asleep as indicated by the string of 'zzzzzzzzzzzz...'. The giant in question is the chalk figure of the Long Man of Wilmington, 235 feet in height, its origins have been the subject of many theories and fanciful folklore. First recorded in a drawing dated 1710, it seems the original figure did once have facial features but was not robbed of his genitalia by prudish Victorians.

Winchelsea

A name first seen in 1130 as Winceleseia, this name comes from old English *wincel eg* and describes 'the island by a river bend'. However, this is not a reference to the location of the present settlement, the original Winchelsea stood on a large shingle bank created by and protecting the confluence of the rivers Brede, Rother, and Tillingham. A document dating from the 1260s records a community of over 700 houses, 50 inns, and two churches. It was of great importance in trade from the Continent, particularly known for the importing of wine from Gascony. During this period it suffered greatly from coastal erosion until, in 1287, a massive flood completely destroyed the place.

This was not a local event. Known as St Lucia's Flood, it occurred on 14 December 1287 and affected all of the coastline of western Europe. A storm surge, created when a high tide coincided with a region of extreme low pressure, broke through sea defences on the day after St Lucia's Day and resulted in casualties which have been estimated as at least 50,000 and may have been as high as 80,000.

Modern or New Winchelsea was a planned town ordered by Edward I which inherited all the titles and charters of its predecessor. Winchelsea has both a mayor and corporation making it a candidate for the smallest town in Britain, although this is disputed by several other small towns.

Camber Castle gets its name from *cambra*, not a true Old French term but one Anglicised. Clearly the locals were not overly impressed by this fortification for its name means 'room', used to describe 'a confined space'.

Pubs begin with the modern name of Pub 31, the number is part of the postcode of TN31 which was given to this part of Winchelsea. Its location is also relevant in the name of the Seahorse and, on Sea Road, the Ship Inn. The Bridge Inn marks a crossing point, while the New Inn is a reminder there were already inns here when this was built, although this had not been 'new' since soon after it was constructed in 1778.

Withyham

Telling of 'the hemmed-in land where willow trees grow', this comes from Old English *withig hamm* and is recorded as Withiham in 1230.

Minor place names of the parish include Buckhurst, this 'wooded hill of birch trees' would have made it visible from some distance. Gillridge Farm was established as 'the golden ridge', although whether this referred to flora, the land, or simply because it was well lit is uncertain. Groombridge links Middle English *grome* and Old English *brycg* to refer to 'the bridge of the servant', presumed to be a trusted employee of the lord of the manor who ensured the bridge was in good repair.

The church of St Michael and All Angels was begun in the 13th century, although a major rebuild in the 14th century was necessary to incorporate a chapel for the Sackvilles. On 16 June 1663 the church was hit by lightning and suffered severe damage. Aside from parts of three walls little remained, even the church bells were now lumps of molten metal. Rebuilt by 1672, the original five bells were recast and installed in 1674, a sixth appeared in 1715, and two further bells added in 1908.

Wivelsfield

Records of this name include Wifelesfeld around 765, a name which probably refers to 'the open land of a man called Wifel', where the origin is a Saxon personal name and Old English *feld*. Alternatively the first element could be *wifel*, in which case this would give 'the open land infested by weevils'.

Antye Farm is a place with a name meaning 'at the high', we can only assume this must mean 'at the high farm'. Berth Lane runs past the area known as *baere* 'swine pasture'. Ote Hall features the suffix *halh* describing 'the nook of land of a man called Ohta'.

Common Place Name Elements

Element	Origin	Meaning
ac	Old English	oak tree
banke	Old Scandinavian	bank, hill slope
bearu	Old English	grove, wood
bekkr	Old Scandinavian	stream
berg	Old Scandinavian	hill
birce	Old English	birch tree
brad	Old English	broad
broc	Old English	brook, stream
brycg	Old English	bridge
burh	Old English	fortified place
burna	Old English	stream
by	Old Scandinavian	farmstead
ceap	Old English	market
ceaster	Old English	Roman stronghold
cirice	Old English	church
clif	Old English	cliff, slope
cocc	Old English	woodcock
cot	Old English	cottage
cumb	Old English	valley
cweorn	Old English	queorn
cyning	Old English	king
dael	Old English	valley
dalr	Old Scandinavian	valley
denu	Old English	valley
draeg	Old English	portage

dun	Old English	hill
ea	Old English	river
east	Old English	east
ecg	Old English	edge
eg	Old English	island
eorl	Old English	nobleman
eowestre	Old English	fold for sheep
ersc	Old English	wooded hill
fald	Old English	animal enclosure
feld	Old English	open land
ford	Old English	river crossing
ful	Old English	foul, dirty
geard	Old English	yard
geat	Old English	gap, pass
haeg	Old English	enclosure
haeth	Old English	heath
haga	Old English	hedged enclosure
halh	Old English	nook of land
ham	Old English	homestead
hamm	Old English	river meadow
heah	Old English	high, chief
hlaw	Old English	tumulus, mound
hoh	Old English	hill spur
hop	Old English	enclosed valley
hrycg	Old English	ridge
hwaete	Old English	wheat
hwit	Old English	white
hyll	Old English	hill

lacu	Old English	stream, water course
lang	Old English	long
langr	Old Scandinavian	long
leah	Old English	woodland clearing
lytel	Old English	little
meos	Old English	moss
mere	Old English	lake
middel	Old English	middle
mor	Old English	moorland
myln	Old English	mill
niwe	Old English	new
north	Old English	north
ofer	Old English	bank, ridge
pol	Old English	pool, pond
preost	Old English	priest
ruh	Old English	rough
salh	Old English	willow
sceaga	Old English	small wood, copse
sceap	Old English	sheep
stan	Old English	stone, boundary stone
steinn	Old Scandinavian	stone, boundary stone
stapol	Old English	post, pillar
stoc	Old English	secondary or special settlement
stocc	Old English	stump, log
stow	Old English	assembly or holy place
straet	Old English	Roman road
suth	Old English	south
thorp	Old Scandinavian	outlying farmstead

treow	Old English	tree, post
tun	Old English	farmstead
wald	Old English	woodland, forest
wella	Old English	spring, stream
west	Old English	west
wic	Old English	specialised, usually dairy farm
withig	Old English	willow tree
worth	Old English	an enclosure
wudu	Old English	wood

Bibliography

Beecher, Alan F. (ed.) *The Story Behind Bexhill Street Names* (Bexhill Museum Association, 1996)

Davey, L.S. and Clark, Kim *The Street Names of Lewes* (Pomegranate Press, 2010)

Dunkling, Leslie and Wright, Gordon *A Dictionary of Pub Names* (Routledge & Kegan Paul, 1987)

Ekwall, Eilert *The Concise Oxford Dictionary of English Place Names* (Oxford University Press, 1960)

Barnes, J. Mainwaring *Historic Hastings* (Cinque Port, 1986)

Mawer, A. and Stenton, F.M. *The Place Names of Sussex Pts I & II* (Cambridge, 1969)

Mills, A.D. *Dictionary of English Place Names* (Oxford, 1998)

Milton, John T. *Origins of Eastbourne's Street Names* (Eastbourne Local History Society, 1995)

Rye's Own

Printed in Great Britain
by Amazon